TURN HIM ON...
VIRTUOSO LO...

Once upon a time women were supposed to be
the passive partner in making love—waiting
for the man to make the first move, and
following his lead after that.

Today the rules of the love game have
changed. You no longer have to be afraid to
make him think you enjoy sex *too* much.

Now you can be your own one-woman sexual
extravaganza and make every inch of him an
erogenous zone.

Now you can lust your way into his insatiable
heart with your gloriously wicked blaze of
sexual plenty.

He'll cherish you for it.

MAKING LOVE:
A WOMAN'S GUIDE

POSITIVE ATTITUDES (0451)

☐ **HOW TO BE AN ASSERTIVE (NOT AGGRESSIVE) WOMAN IN LIFE, IN LOVE, AND ON THE JOB—A Total Guide to Self-Assertiveness by Jean Baer.** Learn how to express your opinions and wishes, and stand up for your rights with these revolutionary new techniques of assertiveness training by the co-author of the bestselling *Don't Say Yes When You Want to Say No.* (165225—$5.99)

☐ **WHISPERED SECRETS: *The Couple's Guide to Erotic Fantasies* by Iris and Steven Finz.** Meet couples who shed all semblance of modesty when they are alone together and use fantasy to achieve fulfillment at its most ecstatic. (164016—$4.99)

☐ **FOR EACH OTHER: Sharing Sexual Intimacy by Lonnie Barbach.** This famed psychologist and sex therapist gives the program for the aspects of a relationship—physical and psychological—that affect sexual satisfaction. "New discoveries . . . the best book about female sexuality now available." —*Psychology Today* (152719—$5.99)

☐ **FOR YOURSELF: The Fulfillment of Female Sexuality by Lonnie Barbach.** Here is a unique book that demonstrates in a step-by-step program how you can indeed take control of your life at its most intimate, personal and fundamental level. (166817—$5.99)

☐ **LIFEMATES: *The Love Fitness Program for a Lasting Relationship* by Harold Bloomfield, M.D. and Sirah Vettese, Ph.D., with Robert Kory.** "Fantastic! Brilliant strategies and practical insights."—Ken Blanchard, co-author of *The One Minute Manager.* (171721—$5.50)

Prices slightly higher in Canada

Buy them at your local bookstore or use this convenient coupon for ordering.

NEW AMERICAN LIBRARY
P.O. Box 999, Bergenfield, New Jersey 07621

Please send me the books I have checked above.
I am enclosing $_____ (please add $2.00 to cover postage and handling). Send check or money order (no cash or C.O.D.'s) or charge by Mastercard or VISA (with a $15.00 minimum). Prices and numbers are subject to change without notice.

Card #_____ Exp. Date _____
Signature_____
Name_____
Address_____
City _____ State _____ Zip Code _____

For faster service when ordering by credit card call **1-800-253-6476**

Allow a minimum of 4-6 weeks for delivery. This offer is subject to change without notice.

MAKING LOVE:
A Woman's Guide

by
Judith Davis

A SIGNET BOOK

SIGNET
Published by the Penguin Group
Penguin Books USA Inc., 375 Hudson Street,
New York, New York 10014, U.S.A.
Penguin Books Ltd, 27 Wrights Lane,
London W8 5TZ, England
Penguin Books Australia Ltd, Ringwood,
Victoria, Australia
Penguin Books Canada Ltd, 10 Alcorn Avenue,
Toronto, Ontario, Canada M4V 3B2
Penguin Books (N.Z.) Ltd, 182–190 Wairau Road,
Auckland 10, New Zealand

Penguin Books Ltd, Registered Offices:
Harmondsworth, Middlesex, England

Published by Signet, an imprint of New American Library,
a division of Penguin Books USA Inc.

First Printing, January, 1984
15   14   13   12   11   10   9   8   7

Copyright © 1983 by Caroline Latham
All rights reserved

 REGISTERED TRADEMARK—MARCA REGISTRADA

Printed in the United States of America

BOOKS ARE AVAILABLE AT QUANTITY DISCOUNTS WHEN USED TO PROMOTE PRODUCTS OR SERVICES.
FOR INFORMATION PLEASE WRITE TO PREMIUM MARKETING DIVISION, PENGUIN BOOKS USA INC., 375
HUDSON STREET, NEW YORK, NEW YORK 10014.

If you purchased this book without a cover you should be aware that this book is stolen
property. It was reported as "unsold and destroyed" to the publisher and neither the
author nor the publisher has received any payment for this "stripped book."

Contents

Introduction: A "Perfect" Night   9

1 What Do Men Really Want?   15

2 How to Take Charge Without
    Taking Over   22

3 How to Feel Sexy   32

4 Making It Special   40

5 The Spice of Variety   52

6 The Mind as an Erogenous Zone   63

7 Touring the Erogenous Zones   76

8 Your Enjoyment Is His Greatest
    Turn-on   86

9 Sexual Intercourse   96

10 Other Sexual Pleasures   115

11 Timing   131

12 When You Run into Problems   141

13 Erotic Fun and Games   151

14 Some Special Secrets   161

15 Putting It All Together   167

MAKING LOVE:
A Woman's Guide

INTRODUCTION

A "Perfect" Night

How do *you* imagine the perfect night of love?

If you are like most women, it starts with the thrill of a ringing phone. It's Him, and he wants to see you. On the appointed evening, you give yourself plenty of time at the end of the day for a leisurely bath, a change into clothes that make you feel pretty and sexy, clouds of perfume, and a flattering new way to do your hair. When he arrives, he's brought you flowers, and he tells you how lovely you look. Then he sweeps you off to a romantic restaurant, where he has reserved a cozy table for two in the corner. He orders champagne and you toast the evening ahead.

After dinner, he invites you back to his place for a nightcap. There is more champagne stashed in his refrigerator, good music, dim lights. Somehow you find yourself in the bedroom, where he admiringly removes your clothes, caresses you gently, and makes love to you all night long—to the accompaniment of murmurs of gratitude and appreciation. The following morning, he remains attentive. He brings you a cup of coffee before your shower, and offers you breakfast, which he has cooked himself. When you *finally* get in to your office, you find a dozen roses waiting for you, and a warm compliment on the card that almost makes you blush.

What's wrong with this picture?

Sounds perfect, doesn't it? Wouldn't you just love for it to happen to you? But think about this scenario more carefully. All the happiness, all the pleasure, all the perfections of the night are *due entirely to the actions of the imaginary Mr. Right.* Your contribution amounts to nothing more than an ability to appreciate all that he is giving. Other than a certain willingness, you have given nothing of yourself.

The end result of this imaginary evening would certainly be that you always remember him, and the wonderful moment he created in your life. But what will *he* remember? Will he really think of you fondly for the rest of his life just because you were so . . . responsive?

Of course not.

The truth is, this imaginary evening makes a nice daydream, but it is a poor model for real life. If it really happened to you, you probably wouldn't find yourself too happy. One reason is that it is thoroughly selfish. He is doing all the giving, you are doing all the taking. Chances are, if you met a woman who really behaved like that time and time again, your reaction would be the same as most men's: you wouldn't like her very much.

Another problem with this "perfect" fantasy is that the woman's role in it is so passive, so empty. The man in the scenario could presumably do it again the next night, and the next, and the next—as long as his money and his energy held out! But there is nothing special about your presence—you could be replaced by anyone. In addition, you'd have to wait until someone else came along and arranged another wonderful evening. Not only is that not practical (you'd be lucky if you ever ran across *one* of these paragons and two is certainly too much to ask of life), it is also *not desirable*. While the man is actively expressing himself—his interests, his tastes, his personality—you are almost depersonalized. You tell him nothing about your most intimate self, and your part could be played by anyone who possessed the basic quality of willingness.

Really, it's much more fun to play an active part in the proceedings. You'll like yourself better, and you are sure to find that it brings you even greater pleasure.

Take two

Now try to imagine the scenario again—this time with yourself as a *full partner* in the events. Your participation might start when he calls and you suggest returning to *your* place after dinner for dessert and coffee. You could make a lemon pie with the recipe your sister sent and serve it on the new plates you bought because you loved the whimsical designs and cheerful colors. Already the evening is flavored by a bit of your own personality. And when he makes love to you, it will be on the delicate pastel sheets that you have softly scented with lavender, thereby gratifying another of his senses (and yours). After he believes he is exhausted, you can delight him with an initiative of your own that soon revives his interest: a bubble bath for two, followed by a massage that gradually turns into something more urgent. If he's a resourceful man, he'll still be able to fix your breakfast the next morning, even though he is working in an unfamiliar kitchen.

In this new scenario, you'll certainly continue to think about him the next day, and you'll be just as delighted when those roses are delivered to your office. But he will also be thinking about *you*, and the chances are good he will now be looking forward to another evening together just as eagerly as you are. Suddenly the relation-ship is much more balanced, much more excitingly real, and you are really equal collaborators. You each have a memory it took both of you to create.

This doesn't mean that every minute you spend with a man has to be exactly a fifty-fifty proposition: that's not making love, it's some kind of contest. Obviously everyone likes to be spoiled sometimes, and you should allow yourself to be on the receiving end often. But remember that it can be just as nice to give the gift of spoiling another person for a day, or night. The important thing is that there should be some reciprocity. Take turns: if you do have a night like the one in our first scenario, there ought to be a follow-up, in which you are the one doing the giving.

At first, because you may not be used to it, it might take a bit of effort to get into the habit of seeing yourself as a full partner in the delightful process of making love. But it's an effort definitely worth making. Some of the benefits:

- You will boost your self-confidence.
- Your sense of your own worth will be enhanced.
- You will have the opportunity to express your self: your own likes and dislikes, tastes and preferences.
- Your lover's pleasure will be increased.

And therefore:

- Your own pleasure will be increased as well.

This book was written to help you think of more ways to be an active participant in making love with the men in your life. It's not a manual to tell you what's "right" and what's "wrong," and it's not a set of instructions that you have only to follow to achieve guaranteed bliss. It's just some suggestions, perhaps some new ways of looking at things, for you to use as the basis for your own ideas of things that are right for you and your partner. Read on. . . .

CHAPTER ONE

What Do Men Really Want?

As Joan locked her front door behind Steve, she tried to make sense of the evening. She had talked to him a number of times at meetings of the IBM Microcomputer Club, and tonight they had gone out for a hamburger afterward. Then Steve had suggested that he'd like to see her home. When they got to her door, he insisted on coming inside. Then he asked for a drink, and then he tried to seduce her on the living-room sofa. Joan was initially responsive, but as things progressed to greater intimacy she told him that she thought it was a little too early in their acquaintance to go any further, and besides, she was really tired from a long day at the office. Steve had said that he was tired too, and also mentioned that he had a meeting early in the morning. But instead of getting up to go, he kept right on trying. And trying and trying. It got later and later, but Steve wouldn't give up, and finally at about one o'clock in the morning, Joan gave in. She was simply too tired to resist any longer, and after all, she *did* find him attractive, even though she still thought this wasn't really the right time for it. . . .

But when they were at last in bed, Steve suddenly seemed less interested, and at one point in the proceedings, Joan could have sworn that he was about to drop off to sleep. He wasn't a terrible lover, but he was definitely halfhearted. She began to feel that he regarded her more as a responsibility than as a pleasure. So to put an end to the whole lackluster performance, she faked a climax. He seemed relieved and quickly followed suit. After a few minutes, he remarked that he'd better go home: he had to get up early in the morning for that meeting, he had to change his suit, and he didn't want to disturb her. He threw on his clothes and left.

Aftermath: a tragedy in two dialogues

Joan thinks:

Why did Steve insist on making love tonight? Couldn't he see we were both too tired to enjoy it? And how could he be so determined in the living room and so much less inspired in the bedroom? Did I turn him off? But if that's true, why did he go through with it? Was it just for the sake of those few minutes of sex? What did he want from me anyway?

Joan makes herself a comforting cup of tea and thinks sadly that all Steve was interested in was sex. How surprised she would be if she could hear what Steve was saying to himself as he hurried home!

Steve thinks:

How could I have been so dumb? I should have known it was too late, and I was too worried about that meeting in the morning—*I could be fired*—to be any good in bed. But I didn't know how to tell her. And I thought that once I'd come on to her so strong, she would be angry if I didn't finish what I started. She's probably really disappointed in me. . . . I don't know if I'll have the nerve to call her again.

Unfortunately, this sort of misunderstanding is not as rare as it ought to be. Sometimes it's all too easy to be like Joan and conclude that all men are only interested in sex. Don't we hear them boast about their conquests with no sign of involvement with the woman concerned? And what about men's magazines, which seem to be devoted entirely to the Quest for Sex?

The myths about male sexuality

There are certain "truths" that everyone knows.

- A real man will always be immediately aroused by the mere *thought* of sex.
- A real man never fails to take advantage of any opportunity to make love to a woman.

- A real man knows he should never settle for *no* for an answer.
- A real man refuses to be deterred from sex by a mere matter of feelings, either his own or his partner's.

It is a pity that these myths are so prevalent. The worst part is not just that women believe them, but that many men do. These misconceptions often influence a man's behavior, as he tries to live up to what he believes is expected of him. But it's important to realize that they are all *more myth than reality*.

These myths may be what he says when he's talking to the other guys (who are all lying through their teeth to impress each other with their sexual prowess). They may even be what he tries to tell himself, or the way he tries to force himself to behave. But they are not the truth about the male of the human species.

Of course, your lover may sometimes surprise you by the speed of his response and be ready to make love before the thought has even crossed your mind—there's no question that a man's physiological response time is usually faster than a woman's. And he may occasionally be in the mood for a "quickie" when his partner is not, or choose to have sex without any long-term commitment. Those situations can be hard for a woman to accept if she has deeper feelings. But remember: that's a choice more women are also beginning to make as they have the increasing freedom to do so.

Still, no man is a sex machine. Whatever he may claim, he is not merely an appendage of some hot throbbing organ. He is a whole human being and his sexual response is in fact a somewhat complicated and delicate process that is easily influenced by his thoughts, attitudes, and emotions. He may sometimes be too tired for good love-making, or too worried. He may care too much about his partner, or not enough. His feelings may be hurt by something she has said, or something he's afraid she is going to say. He may be frightened that he's not going to get an erection, or that it won't last, or that he won't be able to satisfy his partner.

How to be kind

The kindest thing you can do for any man in your life is to refuse to take these myths seriously. Treat him like a real person, not an escapee from the pages of *Penthouse*. Try to discover how he really feels—and then respect his feelings. When things don't go well between you, don't take the easy way out and mutter that "Men are all alike." Find out what is going on with this particular man at this time. Is he tired but trying not to show it? Is he embarrassed over some awkward move he made and now compensating for it by lunging at you like King Kong going after Fay Wray? Does he really want to make love now or does he just think you expect him to? *Find out!*

Jonathan, a screenwriter in Los Angeles, summed it all up when he tried to answer the question of what men really want. "The nicest thing a woman can do for me is to treat me the way she likes to be treated. What men 'really want' is just the same thing women really want. They want to be respected. They want to be treated well. They want to be recognized as individuals."

This doesn't mean that you have to offer every lover your eternal slavish devotion, nor does it mean that lovemaking should always go exactly the way he wants it, with no input from you. But it does mean that you should not treat your partner like a Typical Man but like another human being with whom you have embarked on the most pleasant and fun-filled of joint ventures. When you stop believing in the myths and the preconceived notions or images and leave yourself open to learning about the needs and desires of the one special man you are with, you open up lots of good possibilities. Relieved of those imagined pressures of performance, your lover will be able to think about what he *really* wants to do. Maybe he'd like close physical contact without sex, just for once; maybe he'd like to cuddle up and fall asleep and save lovemaking for the morning. Or maybe he'd like to escape the burden of always being the one to plan and orchestrate the sexual activities; maybe he'd like to be seduced for a change. Or perhaps he'd like to enact some wild fantasy and pounce on you like a panther in the jungle.

Whatever it is, he is certain to enjoy it more (and help you enjoy it more too) if his thoughts and feelings are in harmony with the rest of his body. Sex is more fun if your partner feels he's not seen as just a functional penis thrusting away but as a real human being with whom you are sharing an important experience.

CHAPTER TWO

How to Take Charge Without Taking Over

"Ed and I have been working on a project together for the last several months," said Gretchen. "I find him a very attractive man, and I'd like to get to know him better outside the office. But I don't know how to make the first move. I keep remembering how we all criticized one of my high-school friends for chasing after a boy in our class. My mother used to say, 'The more she runs after him, the faster he's going to run away.' Maybe times *have* changed . . . but have they really changed that much?"

Many women share Gretchen's hesitation about making the first move. After all, for many years they were taught to be coy, not to say "yes" too quickly—and suddenly they are trying to learn to be the ones who ask the question! Those old rules still have their effect. We no longer wear white gloves every time we leave the house but we still remember some of those rules for behaving like a "lady":

- "A nice girl never calls a boy first."
- "Men don't respect you if you chase them."
- "Throwing yourself at a man is an act of desperation."
- "Men are only interested in you if they think you're hard to get."

It's misleading to call these old sayings myths because, as we have all found out, under certain circumstances they still remain true. Some men *are* still prisoners of these ideas, and they may turn down your approach in a way that will hurt your feelings. But if you are sometimes brave enough to take the risk and make the first move, you will soon find that there are many men out there who respond warmly. They also enjoy the thrill of the chase (and make sure that you sometimes give them that opportunity), but they are tired of having to take all the risks themselves. Despite years of experience and a confident façade, they still worry every time they come on to a woman: *Will she like me? Will she say yes? Or will she think I'm a jerk, tell me to get lost?* How nice for a change to know from the very beginning where they stand!

So the rewards of learning to make the first move can easily outweigh the risks. But there are a couple of points to bear in mind to help make the experience a successful one for you.

Pick a time when the two of you are alone

In the privacy of his own apartment, a man may feel very comfortable with behavior that would embarrass him to death in public. Arthur, a reporter in Houston, explains: "Sure, sometimes I like to lie back and let my girlfriend do all the work—plan the evening we are going to spend and even pay for it. One of the things that attracted me to Sally in the first place was that she seemed so in control of her life; and as far as I am concerned, that can extend to sex as well. But that's something that happens just between the two of us. I'd be uncomfortable with the idea that any of the guys knew about it."

Many men have literally made a lifetime investment in a public image of themselves as people who take charge, exert control; and they will react defensively to any threat to that image in public. They may like the idea of occasionally following orders in bed (or during the process of getting there), but they don't feel the same way about obeying commands issued in public. If you are having dinner together at your apartment, your man may be thrilled to hear you say, "Let's skip dessert and go right to bed; you're better than chocolate cake any day!" But if you tried the same thing in a restaurant, with the waiter standing by and the couple at the next table tuned in, his reaction could be quite different. You can bet a romantic evening would be ruined.

Make sure your approach doesn't have possessive overtones

You may have watched this scenario in a bar or at a party. A woman who apparently has just made a conquest suddenly begins to hang all over the poor man. She openly assumes he is going to pay for her drinks or take her out to dinner. She talks about when "we" are going to leave. She may even go so far as to display jealousy if he strikes up a conversation with some other woman nearby. The result is always the same: somehow she finds herself going home alone.

This sort of self-defeating behavior is often the result of the woman's sense of uneasiness about initiating the action. But remember that if you make the first move toward a man, and he responds, he too may be a little self-conscious about the fact. So it doesn't hurt to bend over backward to recognize his independence and let him take the initiative in other areas. Don't assume that his presence in your bed means you can decide all by yourself when he is going home or when you are going to see him again. Regardless of which of you has made the first move, the relationship, as long as it lasts, still should be something close to a fifty-fifty proposition.

Don't use the situation as a disguise for emotional demands

A young insurance executive said, "Pat invited me to go away for a weekend with her, to her family's vacation house in the country. I like Pat, and I think we could have had a good time together, but I lied and told her I had to stay in town for a Saturday-afternoon business meeting. I was just afraid she was going to jump to the wrong conclusion if I accepted, and right now I don't want to make any further commitment."

When a woman accepts an invitation from a man for drinks and dinner or an evening at the theater, she fears that her acceptance will lead him to conclude he can make sexual demands on her. When a man accepts a similar invitation from a woman, his fear is that the subsequent demands will be emotional ones. It would seem that such a fear is not completely unrealistic; many women do indeed secretly hope that the time spent together under the conditions they have carefully arranged will lead to increased love and commitment. The problem is not so much with the woman's secret motivation as it is with her behavior. She will be most successful if she is careful to avoid the appearance of any such demands or assumptions. She must make it clear that she is asking him only for an evening, or day, or weekend of his time—during which both partners can be expected to treat one another with some degree of affection and a lot of respect. He should understand that if he agrees to her request, it will not be interpreted as a commitment to anything other than being a good companion.

Interestingly, once a woman makes a man feel certain that there will be no hidden demands, thus allowing him to relax and enjoy the moments they spend together, it may very well turn out that he is one who is looking for an increased commitment to such a wonderful woman!

Learn when to stop

Just as important as knowing how to take the initiative is knowing when you should stop doing it. No relationship can survive for long if it is really one-sided, no matter who has been the instigator. The key is *balance*. If you were the one to suggest getting together, let him be the one to make the first move toward lovemaking. Or if you suggested making love, give him the chance to take the lead once you get to bed. On an evening when he takes you out, surprise him by being the sexual aggressor in bed. But don't do *everything*. Making the first move doesn't mean that you have to make all the moves; leave plenty of room for his participation.

And although you should learn to feel self-confident about making the first move in a new relationship, think carefully about making the second. If he doesn't reciprocate your first approach, it is probably not wise to try again; the chances are you'll wind up feeling hurt and rejected. In a long-term relationship, you might allow more leeway. If you know that he's been very busy, or short of funds, or upset over something else that's happening in his life, you might reach out to him three or four times in a row. But sooner or later the accounts have to be balanced. This insistence is not a sign of selfishness on your part, but wisdom in realizing that an unbalanced relationship is not good for either party. He will feel that you are pushing him, you will feel that he is using you; the resentment always surfaces in time, and things between you are no longer so comfortable.

More and more men are discovering just how nice it can be when a truly feminine woman has the self-confidence to make the first move. So if you feel you're ready to take the initiative, take control, and make your desires known, consider some of the following possibilities:

• Give him a compliment on his appearance. Tell him he has beautiful hands or a wonderful haircut or the jaw of a male model . . . nothing *too* graphic. It's all a way of making the point that you notice, and appreciate, the physical man.

• Look at him, directly and frequently. The ancient Greeks thought the eyes were the windows of the soul. Remember: sustained eye contact can be a powerful erotic signal.

• Plan an evening together doing something he is really interested in: the annual boat show, a gallery exhibit of photographs of bridges, the screening of an old movie you know he likes, a good college basketball game. He will respond to the fact that it was obviously chosen just for him.

• Send him one elegant masculine flower. New York's Southflower Market suggests a single anthurium (ever noticed how phallic they are?) in a shiny black ceramic vase, or a huge amaryllis in a wine carafe he can reuse, or a tightly budded dark blue iris in a low Japanese bowl.

• Give him your undivided attention. Don't look for the bartender to order another drink, or check out what's on television, or try to locate someone else you know. Focus just on him.

• Ask for his advice (but no personal problems, please). What's a good birthday present for your younger brother, the football nut? How should you mount your stereo speakers for best results? Where can you take your visiting parents for dinner? It's an easy way to get a conversation going; and if he's interested, he can turn it into an opportunity to volunteer further assistance.

• Arrange a surprise treat when you're *not* there. Send him breakfast (there are services that do this, or you could even pack a hamper yourself and dispatch it by taxi) on his first day back after a trip. Leave a pack of his favorite, hard-to-find imported cigarettes on his desk. Have a basket of balloons delivered to mark a business coup. These are perfect first moves because they give him the freedom to choose from a wide range of responses without hurting your feelings: a nice thank-you note may mean he's not interested, but an immediate call to suggest thanking you in person means he is.

• Send him body-language signals. The sexiest posture, say the experts, is a relaxed, "open" one. Keep your arms at your sides rather than crossed in front of you to form a barrier. Lean toward him rather than away. Keep your legs uncrossed but let your knees point in his direction. Recent research shows that couples who are interested in one another tend unconsciously to mirror one another's posture and gestures; for example, he rests his head on his right hand and shortly thereafter, she does the same with her left. Try doing this *consciously* and rely on his subconscious to pick up the message.

Whatever you choose as your first move, do it with confidence and assurance. And don't worry that men will find you too aggressive; after all, it's only the woman who is comfortable with herself and her femininity who can take such a step. Self-confidence is the biggest turn-on of them all.

CHAPTER THREE

How to Feel Sexy

One important ingredient of the self-confidence that can help you take charge is your own sense of being a sexy lady. Consider the following true story.

Lois worked as a waitress in San Francisco's hottest new bar/restaurant. The hours were long, and even with tips the money wasn't great. But she thought she was lucky to have her job, because sooner or later every attractive single man in the city stopped in for a drink. After several months, her love life hadn't really improved that much, but at least she felt certain that she was in the right place for lightning to strike.

One day Lois's fifty-three-year-old aunt, who was visiting from out of town, called to say she thought it would be fun to come see where Lois worked. Lois tried to talk her out of it because she knew her aunt would be too old to fit in with the trendy crowd that frequented the place, but her aunt insisted on dropping in that very evening. Lois kept an eye on the door and rushed up to greet her aunt as soon as she arrived. One glance convinced her that poor Aunt Elizabeth was in for a lonely hour at the bar. She didn't manage to look one second younger than her age: her hair was peppered with gray (and not even attractively styled); her face was lined; she already had a trace of an old woman's mustache; and her figure was stick-thin, with nary a curve in sight.

Almost unconsciously, Lois ran her hand over her own heavy chestnut hair, cut in the latest fashion, and smoothed her uniform down over her enviable figure. She was glad *she* was still young enough to make the effort to look her best—not like her aunt, who apparently no longer cared what men thought when they looked at her. With a kindly manner, Lois settled her aunt at the bar, ordered her a drink, and asked her to wait a few minutes while she arranged to have someone cover for her at her tables. Fifteen minutes later, she rushed back, expecting to find her aunt alone and ignored by the other drinkers at the bar. To her immense surprise, Lois could hardly fight her way through the crowd (mostly men) clustered around her aunt Elizabeth. She was virtually holding court, telling stories about her recent trip to China and her past as a scriptwriter in the last great days of the studio system at MGM. Her audience was attentive and admiring, and they competed with one another to buy her drinks and light her cigarettes. When Lois joined the throng, she was greeted politely but without any particular enthusiasm; despite her youth and good looks, attention remained firmly riveted on her aunt.

When Aunt Elizabeth was ready to leave the bar, she ended up going on to dinner with an absolutely gorgeous hunk in his late twenties whom Lois had had her eye on for weeks. Lois waved good-bye in stunned silence. She couldn't begin to understand what had just happened.

Lois is one of those women—and there are a lot of us—who make the mistake of hoping some man will notice how attractive she has made herself and therefore conclude that she is sexy. Her aunt Elizabeth, an older and wiser woman, has learned not to take the cue from the outside. She knows that the only really important thing is to feel sexy *herself*.

Why self-improvement is not sexy

Many women like Lois, who feel somewhat insecure about whether or not men find them sexy, attempt to cure the problem by embarking on some program that will eradicate what they see as their faults. They will lose ten pounds, or get rid of the saddlebags on their thighs, or take dancing lessons to learn to move more gracefully. They will get a new haircut or try a new makeup. They will have plastic surgery to fix their noses or get silicone injections to smooth away their wrinkles or enlarge their breasts. Then at last they will be attractive—and therefore sexy. The odd thing about this seemingly logical approach is that what it generally leads to is the perception of yet another flaw that must be tackled immediately. As soon as you have a really good hairstyle, you decide your hair is the wrong color and must have expert salon frosting. Losing ten pounds reveals that you have a flabby waistline or cellulite thighs.

Have you ever noticed how it is often the women with the most enviable looks who are also the most truly anguished over their shortcomings? A recent biography of Elizabeth Taylor revealed that the reason she was so often late for appointments was that after she was all dressed and ready to go, she would catch sight of herself in the mirror and decide that she looked too awful to appear in public; so she would spend another hour frenziedly trying to find a dress she thought looked good on her or a hairdo that was more becoming. If the twenty-five-year-old Elizabeth Taylor could be so convinced she was still not attractive enough, what hope is there for the rest of us?

No, the surprising truth of the matter is that feeling sexier will probably not come from some self-improvement campaign. That doesn't mean they don't work, or that you should never undertake them. They can give you very specific benefits: increased physical fitness, more manageable hair, a firmer derriere. But that doesn't necessarily make you feel any more attractive—

and it certainly doesn't guarantee you'll be one whit sexier. In fact, it is often the case that trying to make yourself conform to some ideal of physical beauty may have exactly the opposite effect and make you feel *less* sexy. It can make you preoccupied with your flaws and therefore less secure. It can make you self-absorbed, which is the very antithesis of what's sexy. And worst of all, it can reinforce the erroneous notion that sexiness is a label you receive when men look at you in a certain way rather than a quality you have within yourself.

What does it mean to be sexy?

"Sexy" is not a synonym for beautiful. It doesn't mean being fashionable, chic, or well dressed. In fact, most men agree that clothes have little or nothing to do with it! Sexy means *interested in sex.* Bill, a professor at a college in Massachusetts, says, "To me, a sexy woman is one who conveys an impression of sexual possibilities. Maybe nothing will happen; sexy women aren't necessarily more available than others, and in fact they are often less so. But you know that, even if it's just for a minute, they've really thought about you as a lover. They've imagined the possibility." He goes on to add, "It's a real turnoff to realize that a woman is more concerned with how she looks than with how you make her feel."

Bill's distinction between sexual interest and sexual availability is worth bearing in mind. Being sexy means having a healthy interest in the delights of sexual experience; it doesn't mean being a mobile, bottom-wiggling invitation to ecstasy. You can develop and express your sexuality without being obliged to go to bed with all the men you find appealing. Sexiness is a feeling that lies within yourself. Deciding what to do with it is a choice to make carefully, on the basis of your feeling about the situation and the man in question.

A sexy woman appreciates her own body. Instead of concentrating on your flaws (and you know that even Perfect 10s have them), think about your assets. What is there about you that a man would enjoy when he makes love to you? Perhaps you have the elegant high-arched feet of a classical Greek statue, or smooth soft skin that invites a caress. If you feel that you are plump by today's standards, think of yourself as one of those wonderful voluptuous pink-and-white nudes by Renoir, some of the sexiest ladies ever set on canvas. Or if you think you are too thin to measure up to *Playboy* standards, ask yourself how many of those playmates have your miraculously tiny waist that even Audrey Hepburn might envy.

A sexy woman enjoys all kinds of sensual gratifications. Encourage yourself to luxuriate in the world of the senses. Listen to the faint rustle of a little silk teddy and notice the way it slithers over your skin. Bask in the cozy softness of a fluffy mohair coat. Inhale the scent of your bubble bath and feel the way the warm fragrant water laps over your body. Appreciate the cool fresh comfort of all-cotton sheets in the summertime or the warmth of flannel sheets in the winter. Many women who live alone make the mistake of saving their scented candles, huge thirsty towels, and expensive silk nightgowns for the times when they have male visitors. They ought to learn to be just as interested in stimulating and gratifying their own senses.

A sexy woman appreciates men. She really notices the men around her. She sees the beautiful hands of an office coworker, the smoky gray eyes of a neighbor when she meets him at the mail box, the springy athletic stride of the man ahead of her on the sidewalk. Learn to look at men with a connoisseur's taste. If you feel you can carry it off comfortably, you might go on to express your admiration in the form of a compliment, but that's not at all necessary. The important part is to notice and respond to men. That's what gives you the quality of sexiness.

Above all, a sexy woman is interested in sex. This may sound redundant, but in fact it is often the case that a woman's interest in a man is not really sexual. She may want him to give her devotion or admiration; she may want to prove her own desirability to herself or to other people; she may simply want the comfort of being in contact with another human being. There's nothing wrong with any of these desires: it's just that they are not sexual and therefore they have nothing to do with being sexy. Nothing can turn a man on faster than your genuine interest in him as a possible sexual partner, and you don't even need to broadcast it. In fact, it's a message he will pick up even when you attempt to conceal it, and quite often, it's even sexier when you do.

CHAPTER FOUR

Making It Special

In France at the turn of the century, the great courtesans practiced the art of making love memorable. They spent hours deciding what to wear each day, and unlike the fashionable ladies of society, their concern was never with style but with the way their clothes enhanced their appearance. Dresses were chosen to show off a beautiful set of shoulders, a tiny waist; even the colors were those most flattering to the skin. Their underwear was generally more costly than the rest of their outfit—always exquisitely lacy, delicately embroidered, and threaded with fresh ribbons at every wearing. In an age when the pleasures of personal hygiene were still not fully appreciated, these women were meticulous about brushing their teeth and bathing several times a day in costly oils. They also made liberal use of the best French perfume.

But their attention to detail didn't stop with their personal charms. A good courtesan took the same kind of care over her environment. One sent her sheets all the way to Grasse to be laundered, so they could dry in the fresh air that is always lightly scented by nearby fields of lavender. Another was renowned for her carefully trained cook; her lovers swore the best meal in Paris was served in her dining room. Still another made sure her bed pillows were of the very costliest goosedown. Really, it's easy to understand why men were willing to give such women a country estate or a fabulous piece of jewelry just to spend one night of bliss.

Unfortunately, very few of us can devote ourselves exclusively to love and all its niceties. The idea may sound very appealing, but reality intrudes, and we know we'll be damned lucky just to find time to take the sheets out to the laundromat, and the only scent they're likely to have is that of dryer lint! The maid whose duty it is to change the sheets twice a day seems to have vanished, along with the cook who turns out the gourmet suppers at midnight.

But even though we may have very different priorities in our daily lives, there may still be occasions on which we, like the courtesans, want to turn an evening of lovemaking into a memorable occasion ... for our partners and ourselves.

You and the night and the music

"An evening at home with Rob gives me a chance to express another side of myself," says Lisa. "I work in an atmosphere that is strictly tailored suit and good leather briefcase. To succeed in the executive suite, I have to look and act as much like my male counterparts as possible. And most of my dates with Rob, whom I met when we were both in B school, take place in the same atmosphere. We meet somewhere after work, we check our briefcases at the restaurant to have dinner, later we usually go to his apartment because it's closer to the part of town where we both work, and the next morning I have to look as prim and proper as ever as I rush off to an early-morning meeting. So about once a month I love to indulge the purely feminine part of my personality—for my sake as well as Rob's. I spend all day Saturday cooking something I know he likes, spraying perfume on the pillowcases, arranging a centerpiece and candles on the table. Then I slip into something sexy and frilly, and even put a flower in my hair. By the time the doorbell rings, I feel like Scarlett O'Hara as I invite Rhett . . . errr, Rob . . . to come in."

When you are expecting a "gentleman caller," it's fun to devote some planning time and a bit of creativity to preparation. Begin by focusing on the aspect you hope will occupy most of *his* attention: you. This is the time to wear something outrageous, fantastic, even wanton—the sort of thing you'd never have the nerve to wear in public. Ruffles and lace, plunging necklines, see-through fabrics . . . anything goes. And remember, while you're getting dressed, to think about his pleasure in reversing the process. Choose something that's fun to take off!

"I have a cozy, floor-length wool knit dress," says Sarah, "with long sleeves and a high neck, all very unrevealing, *But* . . . there's a long zipper down the front of the dress, and the zipper has a big ring to grab hold of and pull. All the time we were having dinner, he couldn't tear his gaze away from that tantalizing ring."

"I like to wear an antique Victorian blouse," chimes in Katy. "It is very demure, and it has tiny little buttons that run down the front. It takes my boyfriend's clumsy fingers a long time to get them all unbuttoned . . . but you know what they say, getting there is half the fun." Althea customarily chooses a simple flowing caftan; the exciting surprise her lover gets to discover is that underneath she is wearing absolutely nothing.

And while you are planning what to wear, don't forget the little touches that will linger in his memory. Buy the sort of underwear that's called lingerie: a lacy teddy, a pure white cotton camisole, a beribboned garter belt . . . yes, men are still turned on by garter belts and you can find them in expensive lingerie stores or specialty catalogs like the one from Victoria's Secret. Use scented body lotion and spray yourself all over with perfume. Put ribbons or flowers in your hair. Don't forget that some jewelry can be powerfully erotic, with or without your clothes on. Try an ankle bracelet or a long gold chain around your neck with a pendant that dangles seductively near the curve of your breast. (To return to those French courtesans: one of them was famous for never taking off her magnificent string of pearls, and lovers remembered for years the sight of their creamy luster against the glow of her own fair skin.) Be adventurous and go just a little farther than jewelry: put a blush of rouge on your nipples or add a tiny body decal on your derriere. It's a special man, a special night; if you make his fantasies come true, chances are yours will too.

A loaf of bread, a jug of wine

Your lover takes another sip of his cold kir and gazes appreciatively at the ruby-red strawberry floating in his glass. He slips his feet out of his shoes and relaxes happily in a corner of your sofa. He listens attentively to the story of your triumph yesterday in the courtroom and his eyes express his admiration. He sets down his glass, leans gently toward you and . . . *bzzzzzzz*

. . . it's the kitchen timer, which you had set to go off when the roast was done. You leap to your feet to snatch it out of the oven before it is overcooked to a hard dry lump. Frantically you mince some garlic for the sauce, pour the pan juices through a strainer. Ooops! Grease stain on your satin pants, but no time to stop and change because of course the sauce will be ruined if you don't keep stirring constantly.

Fifteen minutes later, you are serving slices of rare roast beef with an elaborate sauce that is perfectly prepared. So what if you are hot, sweaty, and disheveled? Does the greasy stain near your crotch really matter? Will he care that the hand he wants to holds smells like garlic?

What do you think?

The point is that you should carefully consider your choice of a menu on these special occasions shared with your lover. Your goal is to create a relaxed and intimate atmosphere that lends itself to the pleasure of making love, not to win the job of head chef at a gourmet restaurant. It's a good idea to keep the meal on the light side, even if that means leaving him just the least little bit hungry. Don't serve heavy, filling dishes, such as roast beef with dumplings and gravy, or sausage-stuffed cabbage wallowing in sour cream; heavy meals make people want to fall asleep. Other things to avoid: a dinner that makes you work so hard you are exhausted afterward; anything that makes both of you smell like garlic for the next twenty-four hours;

spinach, liver, and anything else his mother might have forced him to eat.

Timing is an important consideration in planning your menu. Don't pick dishes that require precise scheduling in any of their cooking stages, and particularly try to avoid those that call for a flurry of effort just before serving. It is not a good idea to leave your lover all alone and staring moodily out the window for a long stretch of time while you struggle to mash an eggplant or subdue a game hen. (You'll know you've been in the kitchen too long when you hear him on the phone making dates for later in the week!) Good ideas are soups, stews, elegant main-dish salads, anything that can be prepared ahead and served at room temperature or straight out of the refrigerator.

Exercise similar care in your plans for serving alcoholic beverages. You might offer him a few glasses of wine or one cocktail while you're getting dinner on the table . . . more wine with dinner . . . possibly a little brandy with coffee afterward. But don't ply him with drinks or jump up to refill his glass the minute the bottom comes in sight. You want him to be relaxed, not comatose.

The setting for the meal is another detail worth your attention. Flowers and candles, thin wineglasses, pretty china, a tablecloth or place mats: they all contribute to the atmosphere you want to create. Arrange the table so that you sit side by side, or at right angles, rather than across the table from one another. And remember that you don't have to eat the entire meal at the dining table. Serve drinks and nibbles on the terrace porch, or patio, where you can watch the sun go down. Have dessert and coffee on the living-room sofa, or curled up on big cushions in front of a fire.

Obviously it helps to plan ahead. But don't make the mistake of adhering doggedly to your schedule no matter what happens after he gets there. Remember: the most successful dinner of all might be the one you never get to eat!

Postprandial entertainments

Sooner or later, dinner will be over, and you and your guest will start to think about satisfying hungers of a different kind. "I always find this shifting of gears difficult," says Elise. "One minute you are sitting at the table, sipping Sambuca from your best glasses and languidly discussing the movie you saw last week; the next minute you are ripping off each other's clothes. Somehow it seems like there ought to be a smoother transition."

If you too are looking for more graceful ways to handle this transition, consider some of these possibilities:

• Suggest listening to your favorite tape together: relaxed jazz from Bob James, or the wryly modern love songs of Michael Franks, or the classic romantic ballads of Johnny Mathis.

• Curl up together to watch a commercial-free movie on cable or your VCR (naturally, you've selected something romantic, not an action-packed war movie that will have him hanging on every turn of the plot). Or even a TV show on one of the regular networks. The closeness that comes from shared laughter is a terrific aphrodisiac.

• Indulge him in an almost Oriental bath ritual (remember how well this worked in *Shōgun?*). Soap him carefully, with a bar of pine- or mint-scented soap, let him rinse under the shower, and then quickly run a tub of very warm water for him to soak in, with a little pine bath oil. Light candles in the bathroom instead of turning on the strong lights that allow you to see the least little flaw in your makeup, and also bring in your little cassette player with a soothing tape.

• Ask him to rub your neck, shoulders, or back, or brush your hair, or put some lotion on your sunburn . . . you get the idea.

• Read aloud to him, some amusing poetry, or a fairy tale about the prince who woos the princess, or a fun article from a woman's magazine or even something erotic (see Chapter Six for suggestions).

When you finally move into the bedroom itself, it should be a pleasant setting for the lovemaking that will follow. You've probably already put clean sheets on the bed, maybe even sprayed them with your favorite cologne. Make the lighting muted and indirect: a lamp on the far side of the room, a rosy nightlight, flickering candles. Depending on your budget and the extent of your desire to please, you might want to add a few other touches. Fresh flowers or a plant in bloom on a table near the bed, an ice bucket with a bottle of sparkling wine, a freshly laundered robe for him to slip into, satin sheets . . . anything that helps stimulate the senses will add something to your lovemaking.

Once again, don't overlook the decoration of the most important item in the bedroom: you. Many women make the mistake of assuming that once lovemaking is obviously on the agenda, what men really want is total nudity, as quickly as possible. In most cases, that's not true. Your lover will enjoy the chance to watch you undress, and he may even like to see something else underneath. Sexy black stockings held up by lacy garters, a skimpy nightgown, high-heeled mules, a feather boa: don't reject all of these possibilities just because they seem to be clichés. Remember that they got to be clichés for a very good reason, that most men really do enjoy seeing them on women. You can invent your own attire if you want to be creative (one friend says she is certain the reason leg warmers have been selling so well lately is that smart women have discovered their erotic potential). It's often much more titillating to be partially dressed than to be completely undressed.

Send him away with a smile

The end of a special occasion can be just as important as the beginning. If you haven't discussed beforehand when he will leave, it's a good idea to give him a cue: ask him if he would like to stay over for breakfast, or tell him you're sorry you can't ask him to stay because you have conflicting plans. You don't want to offend him by appearing anxious to get him out of the house, nor do you want to alarm him by assuming that he is going to stay forever. Offering him a meal, a snack, one last drink, or a cup of coffee is a friendly gesture; so is taking a shower or bath together before getting dressed to go on your separate ways. Such gestures will smooth the transition back to the concerns of the everyday world in a way that doesn't hurt anyone's feelings.

"I feel that it is especially important to take trouble with your appearance after you get out of bed," comments Sonia, speaking from the experience of several happy long-term affairs. "It's nice to leave a lover with the memory of you looking your best, so I always try to get into the bathroom first, before he gets up. I fix my hair, take off my now-smudged makeup, put on lip gloss, spray on some perfume, and often slip into a pretty robe. So his first sight of me after we make love brings back our lovemaking, and his last sight of me, as we say good-bye at the door, remains a pleasant impression to carry around in his mind while we are apart and remind him how much he would like to come back."

CHAPTER FIVE

The Spice of Variety

"Sure, a comfortable bed is nice," said Mark, "but it's not the *only* place in the world to make love." "How about the bathtub?" put in Perry. "When Helene starts washing my back, I become aroused immediately. There's something about the way the water feels . . . especially when she puts in some of that perfumed bath oil. . . ." "My wife and I still remember the time we made love on the kitchen table before fixing breakfast," contributed Jim. Chris said, "For me, the best place is on a plane. On one of those long flights, when the movie is over and they've turned out the lights, and the stewardess has handed you a blanket and some pillows. You're in your own private world, just the two of you; nobody knows what's happening under there."

These men are talking about one of the secrets of successful lovemaking: the spice of variety. It is an often ignored but extremely easy way to inject new pleasure into a relationship.

When it's a habit, even sex can be boring

It's all too easy for couples to fall into a rigid pattern, dictated by a combination of convenience and habit, that governs their lovemaking. Maybe you always make love in the morning, so you can get up and shower afterward; or always at night, because the children are asleep and the phone doesn't ring. You habitually opt for the comfort of your big bed, for the privacy and seclusion of your bedroom. You think it seems silly to make love on the living-room rug when you only have to take a few steps to get to the softness of a good mattress. You don't like to make love before you go to work because it makes your hair hopelessly frizzy.

These matters of convenience *are* important. However much we may enjoy it, we can't live on love alone, and in addition to the role of lover we may also be worker, parent, neighbor—any number of other roles, each with its own responsibilities. Lovemaking is never very successful when one or both of the partners is fretting over the sales meeting that is scheduled to start in less than an hour, or that day's responsibilities.

But a constant focus on convenience can destroy all sense of romance. It dampens spontaneity and makes love seem like just another bothersome activity that somehow has to be scheduled into an already busy existence. Don't insist on being practical *all* the time. The love-making that occurs at the "wrong" time or in the "wrong" place may turn out to be the most memorable of all. And some of those other concerns may not really be as urgent as you thought they were. Surely there are some days that you can be half an hour late to work without any real damage being done . . . and if you take the phone off the hook for a while, people will call back . . . and is it really the end of the world if the neighbors *do* suspect that you and your husband actually (gasp) make love?

The truth is that men especially love a sense of variety in lovemaking; and they appreciate the women who help them achieve it. "Marilyn is just great," commented Stan. "In the three years we've been together, she's never once said, 'Oh, no, not here.' And believe me, we've made love in some pretty weird places. We tried it in a hammock under some palm trees on a Caribbean island—and did I look ridiculous when I fell out! Once it was on a fishing boat, once it was in the backseat of a friend's car while it was parked in his garage. It doesn't always work out . . . but we have a lot of fun experimenting."

Perhaps men long for variety in the time and place of lovemaking because they are flattered by the notion that your passion is so urgent it can't wait for convenience. Or could it be that it appeals to their sense of adventure? Or maybe it's the thrill of doing something they're not supposed to, like little boys in the cookie jar. Whatever the reason, he'll be pleased if you exhibit a willingness to try new places and times, and this is especially important in sustaining the bloom of a long-term relationship. Even the most devoted man will find that he is less than inspired if the circumstances of lovemaking are always the same. And now that you think about it, don't you feel the same way? No matter how much you enjoy your partner, there's something a little dreary about knowing you are going to make love *every* Wednesday night after you watch the news, or *every* Sunday morning before you fix brunch. And worse yet is the fact that you may begin to assume that you won't make love anytime in between!

"But who knows where or when?"

You may think you already know the perfect time and place to make love, and you may even be right. But remember that even perfection can be boring if it is repeated over and over. So use your imagination and come up with something just a little bit different every now and then. Here's how.

The easiest change to bring about in your lovemaking pattern is the time of day. If you live together, consider times like Saturday afternoon—you don't *always* have to do your errands then—or early Sunday evening, instead of watching *60 Minutes* every week of your life. Suggest taking a shower together at the end of the day's work and let that lead to lovemaking before dinner instead of following your usual pattern and waiting until you're going to sleep at night. Making love just before you fall asleep can be nice and undoubtedly convenient, but remember that it's the time when both of you are probably at your lowest ebb of energy; you may be very pleasantly surprised at what happens when you switch to another time of day.

You might take a tip from the French and consider the possibility of a matinee; they can be very romantic occasions. Invite him over for lunch. (But don't plan to spend too much time actually eating! An omelet, a salad, and a glass of wine is just enough.) You can spend a wonderful hour in bed together and still get back to the office before those people who are indulging in a long business lunch. And the chances are that you'll also be in a better mood!

Now that you've thought of some new times for making love, you can also exercise your creativity in coming up with some new places. Even if you stay inside your own familiar dwelling, you ought occasionally to break the habit of heading straight for the bed. Remember, human beings are adaptable enough to make love in even the most unlikely circumstances, and sometimes the thrill of the challenge makes it all the more interesting. Begin by simply looking for other spots in your bedroom. Do you have a big armchair or a chaise? A furry rug by the bed? Then move on to the bathroom, which is also full of possibilities . . . especially these days, with the trend toward bigger bathrooms with more luxurious furnishings. A shared bath or shower is always a sexy prelude, and sometimes may even become the main event.

The kitchen may seem at first glance an unlikely place to make love—and certainly, in many apartment kitchens today, only a contortionist could manage it. But psychologists tell us that there is a strong emotional connection between food and sex, and everyday experience confirms the fact that being in the kitchen with a woman is a turn-on for many men. More than one romance has begun with stolen kisses in the kitchen during a party; and did you ever notice how frequently men turn amorous while you are cooking dinner? If you have the room for it, consider installing a small settee with pillows or a large comfortable old chair. A love-in kitchen might be a lot more fun than the eat-in type!

No doubt the possibilities of the living room, with its rugs and couches, have already occurred to you. And dining-room banquettes, should you be fortunate enough to have them. There's the overstuffed chair in the study . . . the lounge chairs on the patio or terrace . . . all it takes is a little imagination.

Of course, the most imaginative approach of all is: leaving home. Many couples find that vacations are very romantic interludes, possibly because in the process of getting away they have also broken the patterns of habit in their love-making. Although real vacations may be once-a-year occurrences, how about a weekend in the country? Or even an overnight stay in a hotel: in many cities, luxury hotels have special Saturday-night rates that make them very afford-able. You don't even have to go to another city—a friend in San Francisco treated her boy-friend on his birthday to a night at the Stanford Court Hotel, with champagne on ice when they checked in and all meals brought up from room service. She reported later that he definitely rose to the occasion!

But even when the budget can't cover a single night in a modest hotel, there are still some intriguing possibilities. Angelo had volunteered to look after his neighbors' plants while they were away, and Beth decided to go along with him one evening. "Something about being in those unfamiliar surroundings with him was just very very sexy. Suddenly we found we couldn't keep our hands off one another, and there we were, making love on the living-room sofa. Three days later, when the begonias needed more water, we were back again . . . and this time we had a bottle of wine and our favorite tape to put on their cassette player. Sure, we could have done the same thing at my place, but somehow this was more fun. It was like a game . . . like playing house."

Obviously, you can't really *plan* this sort of experience; its chief charm lies in the fact that it happens spontaneously and infrequently. Your lover will be agreeably surprised if you arrange to borrow a friend's apartment near his office one afternoon, for a few stolen hours of love. But if you plan to do it every Wednesday at two, it becomes just another item on his busy calendar. The secret is to be open to and flexible about the opportunities that come along— possibly even to invent some—but to avoid routinizing them.

"No one will be watching us; why don't we do it in the road?"

"I used to think it was just a poor sense of timing," said Carol. "The summer Renny and I rented a house on the shore, he always seemed to be overcome by passion when we were out on the beach. I wanted to wait until we got back to the house, but he insisted on making love there and then. I thought he was just oblivious to the fact that someone might come along and see us; finally it dawned on me that he was perfectly aware of the possibility and that it added a little spice to the situation for him."

Although it is always dangerous to generalize about differences between the sexes, many women confirm Carol's conclusion. Men frequently seem to find the thought that someone might see the two of you making love a real stimulant, whereas women tend to be somewhat less turned on by the prospect. Although your partner presumably doesn't *really* want to make love to you at high noon on Main Street, he may find certain semipublic places irresistible. The backseat of a taxi, a conference room supposedly not in use, a lounge chair by the swimming pool—such improbable locations seem to fan the flames.

If you feel really uncomfortable with the idea of making love anywhere except behind a securely locked door, say so: neither of you will enjoy the experience if you try to go through with something that makes you tense and anxious. But maybe you can compromise. For example, you could make love on the beach, but be careful to choose a time or place that makes *you* feel that it's unlikely you'll be observed. Or invite him on a picnic in a spot you've carefully selected for its seclusion. With a little willingness on your part, you may find that you grow to like such adventures.

Four scenarios for taking him by surprise

Here, gleaned from interviews, are some proven ideas that just might inspire you to create your own surprises.

1. You make a date for lunch with your lover, suggesting casually that you will "pick up a couple of sandwiches" on your way over to his office. When you arrive, close the door of his office firmly behind you and suggest that he tell his secretary to hold his calls. Unpack your briefcase or canvas bag and lay out the wine (don't forget a couple of plastic glasses), your homemade spicy chicken wings, raw vegetables, and your special dip. Midway through the meal, move onto his lap and share the same carrot stick. Let him make the exciting discovery that underneath your tailored business clothes you are wearing . . . nothing whatsoever. You can be certain he will supply the correct ending to this story.

2. After the two of you have been out for dinner, you take the wheel of the car and drive out to the beach (or the lake). Take off your shoes and wade along the shore; then suggest taking off your clothes and going skinny-dipping. Once you are in the water, stay close to him; let your bodies sway together in the waves. The feeling of warmth when you touch each other will strike an instant spark, and floating there you will be able to achieve and hold positions that would be sheer agony on dry land. The water makes your movements naturally slow and languorous, so your lovemaking will seem almost dreamlike. . . .

3. Ask your boyfriend to join you Saturday morning for a two-mile run or a set of tennis (or any other sport the two of you enjoy). Hot and

sweaty, the two of you return to your apartment. You whisk him right into the shower, where you wash him *all over* with a fresh cake of sandalwood soap. Afterward, hand him a big fluffy bath sheet to wrap up in and guide him gently to the bedroom. Put on a soothing tape, hand him a tall iced glass of something cool to drink and have him lie down while you give him a massage. You begin to smooth a sweet-smelling oil over his back, trace the long muscles of his body with firm fingers, and then slowly, gently, your touch turns into a caress, and he turns over to sweep you into an urgent embrace.

4. You wake up in the middle of the night and turn toward your quietly sleeping husband. Lightly, you stroke his stomach, his thighs, finally his penis . . . your goal is to arouse him without awakening him. When he is fully erect, slip on top of him. He will wake up to find his favorite dream coming true, and his happy response will make the rest of your night's sleep filled with lovingly sensuous dreams.

CHAPTER SIX

The Mind as an Erogenous Zone

Harriett and Jim are dining in one of the city's most fashionable restaurants to celebrate his biggest real estate sale ever—a ten-million dollar office building. Harriett is elegantly dressed in a ladylike Halston that only hints at the sexy figure underneath. The couple sips an expensive bottle of Mouton Rothschild, waiting for their rack of baby lamb to be served by the white-gloved waiters. During a lull in the conversation, Harriett casually reaches over to the bread basket and selects a breadstick, one of the short thick ones covered with sesame seeds, leans toward Jim, and says, "Tonight, when we get back to my place, the *real* celebration will begin. I am going to take off all my clothes. Piece by piece. First my dress, then my slip, my stockings, and finally my panties. . . . Then I'll strip you naked and touch every part of you."

Jim can't believe what he is hearing. He looks happily at the bewitching creature sitting across the table . . . it really *is* going to be a wonderful evening.

"We'll lie down together on the bed. First I will kiss you all over. *All over*, mmm . . . understand? Not an inch of you will be allowed to escape my lips! Then, you know what I'm going to do?" Harriett slowly lifts the breadstick to her lips. Slowly she pushes it in her mouth. Slowly she pulls it back out again. By this time, Jim is ardently appreciative. When the waiter finally arrives with the lamb, he cancels their dessert order and asks for the check as soon as they finish eating. They leave shortly thereafter, hurrying home to carry out Harriett's agenda. It is a night they will both remember.

The power of imagination

Harriett understands one of the most important aspects of lovemaking. The sexiest part of the human body is *the brain*. *Thinking* about sex is the biggest turn-on of all.

You may have experienced the negative side of this power of the mind. When a man is worried about his finances or under stress at work, he may become sexually unresponsive, even when all other conditions are ideal. Some men (and women) have the same problem when they feel guilty about an aspect of the relationship, or in some way pressured by it. No amount of kissing or caressing will arouse a person whose mind is absorbed by something else.

But the positive side is just as powerful. Imagination is always the key to truly satisfying love. So why not harness that power and use it to enhance your man's response?

Carl, an advertising executive, said, "I like it when women talk about sex. But so many of them are shy, almost prudish, when it comes to conversation. They'll enjoy making love but they won't talk about it."

One reason for this reluctance may be that women tend to associate any sort of explicit reference to lovemaking with pornography, which can certainly be exploitative of women. Not many women want to encourage a viewpoint that looks at the female strictly in terms of her sexual characteristics or that makes anyone—man or woman—into nothing more than a sex object.

But it is possible to be sexually explicit without being pornographic. And if you use erotica as a shared experience to pave the way for high-quality lovemaking, there's definitely nothing exploitative about it.

Anne used to be annoyed when she noticed "girlie" magazines in Brian's apartment. Somehow, the sight of all those fabulously endowed women cavorting across the pages made her feel like they were her rivals. "Things between Brian and me are pretty good," she said at the time. "Why does he need those magazines when he already has me?"

But gradually Anne learned that Brian looked

at the magazines simply because they turned him on. They were not a substitute for Anne but a way to think about making love to her. When she began to show a willingness to share the experience with him, he responded with gratitude and affection, and their lovemaking took on an added spark.

You can do it even if you're shy

Not every woman can be as uninhibited as Harriett or Anne. You may feel uncomfortable or even cheap when you talk openly about sex to a man. Don't worry; it's not necessary to do anything that makes you even the slightest bit embarrassed. But it might help to use a little ingenuity to find your own ways of bringing up the subject of sex in a manner that is both fun and inviting. There are lots of tasteful ways to appeal to a man's imagination that require nothing more daring than some advance planning. Consider these options as a way to communicate a healthy and secure sexuality:

- Frame a sexually explicit print or drawing and hang it on your bathroom wall.
- Slip a record of songs about sex on the turntable just after the romantic Sinatra ballads.
- Buy a small erotic statuette and put it on the table beside your bed. (Rodin's "The Kiss" may

be so well known that it's corny, but it still *works*.)

- Put a sexy little book under his pillow. The Japanese actually call these "pillow books" and consider them a classic tradition in literature.

If you feel a bit more daring, you might try to add a more personal touch. You could make a special tape by reading aloud some erotic poems (do it late at night, when you feel relaxed, and your voice will have a husky, intimate quality). Then put it on your stereo or pop it in his Walkman. Or ask him to help you choose a new nightgown from one of those supersexy catalogs like Victoria's Secret; he'll love imagining you in the various skimpy garments (and, another plus, you'll get some insight into his personal tastes and preferences about things like G-strings, black garter belts, and see-through nighties).

Even the great masters do it

Some of the greatest masters have produced sexually explicit works that are both artistic and extremely stimulating. For example, Picasso produced a number of prints and drawings of couples making love. D. H. Lawrence wrote love scenes in *Lady Chatterley's Lover,* a classic, that are more arousing than any of the more recent accounts of who puts what where. And the photogrpahs of Helmut Newton or Jean-Paul Goude are museum-quality work that just happen to have a sexual theme.

You don't want to turn your house into a museum of the erotic, but a few items, discreetly displayed, will provoke your man's imagination. You needn't go to sex shops or dirty-book stores—in fact, you definitely shouldn't if you are looking for the best quality. Many bookstores and museum shops will carry the sorts of things you are looking for—and if you're too shy to take your purchase up to the cash register, try using catalogs. You can request them from museums, from many bookstores, and from mail-order houses.

If you run short of ideas of your own, turn to the end of this chapter for a list of twenty guaranteed turn-ons.

Remember television too. If you have cable TV, there may be a station that plays very sexy movies late at night; your man might be thrilled at the suggestion that you watch it together. (A number of hotels offer this service as well; check the information in your room when the two of you are traveling.) Another possibility is video cassettes. Any store that carries them usually has a section of erotic movies on tape; and if your lover is one of those electronics buffs who always has the most up-to-date equipment, surprise him with a present of the tape of *Last Tango in Paris* (and a bottle of wine) or something similar. A friend with a personal computer says there are even erotic software programs!

Get personal

Of course, the very best way to enlist your lover's imagination is through the personal approach. Can you draw? Tell a story or a sexy joke? Then you can create a way to share your lovemaking even when you are not in bed together. Try writing a little verse about a moment you shared. Or put it in the form of a story: tell about the first time you made love or a particularly good weekend. One friend with a good sense of humor put together a little book written like a gradeschool primer: "See Dick go. Go, Dick, go!"

If words fail you, try drawing a picture instead. Remember, it doesn't have to be a work of art: you're not attempting to please a critic but a lover. It can be as naive as a child's drawing and it will still tell him that you enjoy his lovemaking and encourage him into even greater responsiveness. All you have to do is provide the raw materials and let his imagination do the rest.

Jeannie and Beth found their own novel approach. They got together one evening after work; Beth supplied the makeup and the lingerie, Jeannie the frilly bedroom and the Polaroid. Taking turns, each girl made herself up, tried on a variety of lacy underwear (what there was of it), and posed sitting up in bed, lying down on her stomach, climbing under the sheets, while the other one snapped away with the camera. They were a little shy at first, but then they began to get into the spirit of the project, and by the time they were finished they had used two rolls of film. Jeannie used one of her photos the very next week, pasting it inside a homemade Valentine that she gave her lover when they went out for drinks. Beth placed hers in an outrageously campy frame she found in an antique store and put it on Mike's bedside table the next time she was in his apartment. (Several months later, Mike gave her a beautiful silver frame from Tiffany's; behind the glass was only a little note that said, "Fill me, please.")

Reach out and touch someone

If you remember to appeal to the power of the imagination, then even the times that you are apart can be an extension of your lovemaking. A few years ago, Rickie Lee Jones had a hit song called "Makin' Love on the Phone," and it's still a good idea. Call him at work (but only when you are sure he'll be alone and not distracted by business worries). Call him at home when you're on that business trip. Call him before bedtime on an evening you haven't spent together. Tell him you wish he was there ... and just exactly why. Describe yourself as you are lying in bed; tell him what you are wearing (or what you are not wearing). Be his own personal telephone fantasy. The next time you see him, your reunion will be better than ever.

And don't forget letters either. A short note on beautiful pastel stationery, perhaps just lightly scented with your favorite perfume, is a wonderful surprise in his mailbox every now and then (and if you have any of those photos left over, you might tuck one inside). To make it most effective, keep it brief—just a few erotic sentences that you know will turn him on.

Whether it's a letter or a phone call, use your own language of love. Nothing is more powerful than the names you invent for one another and for your lovemaking; it's one of the most effective forms of communication. One couple speaks of making love as "playing tummy games"; another calls it "being mommy and daddy." Ben tells Celia he wants to visit her dolly's house, and she sometimes playfully refers to his penis as "that masked man." Other people's names for these things always sound silly, but your own are part of the context of your shared pleasures, and just hearing them can make you shiver in delighted remembrance—and anticipation.

Whether you use private words or published ones, candid Polaroid snaps or Picasso etchings is not important. What *is* important is to remember to include that most powerful of all erogenous zones, the mind, in your lovemaking.

TWENTY GUARANTEED TURN-ONS

1. *Sleepless Nights* by Helmut Newton. A book of photographs by the man responsible for *White Women* (and some of *Vogue*'s most innovative photography) that men seem to find irresistible.

2. "Kiss Kiss Kiss" from Yoko Ono's album *House of Glass*. Her piping monotone and erotic suggestions combine very effectively.

3. *The Delta of Venus* by Anaïs Nin. This gifted writer turned to pornography when she was down and out in Paris and created this wonderful book of lewd stories.

4. *Deep Throat*. This classic X-rated film is available on video cassettes.

5. *Japanese Nights.* A portfolio of reproductions of some of the most famous Japanese erotic prints, available in many Japanese import stores as well as some large bookstores. Do what the Japanese do: set up a frame on a little easel by your bed and change the picture inside every week.

6. *Bad Girls.* This Donna Summers album from 1979 is still available in record stores. If he likes a good disco beat coupled with some very erotic lyrics and vocal tricks, this is sure to drive him to new heights.

7. *A Man with a Maid,* by Anonymous. Told in a way that is amusingly archaic, this story seems to cover every possible variety of sexual activity.

8. *Indian Temple Sculptures.* A lavish four-color

coffee-table book about the famed erotic temple sculptures of northern India. Only a contortionist could attempt these positions in real life, but they do have an inspiring effect.

9. *African Fertility Figures.* Reproductions of these clay and metal statuettes are sold in many museum shops, and the real thing occasionally turns up in antique stores for prices that have not yet reached the ridiculous.

10. *The Sly One.* A vintage album by Redd Foxx who is well known for his extremely risqué live performances. It's wonderfully funny comedy that also happens to be very sexy.

11. *The Erotic Drawings of Fragonard.* Step back into eighteenth-century France, when games of love were being invented and refined. The pages are full of cheerfully lascivious lovers, unsuspecting cuckolds, and impudent youths against a background of gardens, forests, and elegantly furnished bed chambers.

12. *The Pearl.* A collection of Victorian erotica, that can be found in paperback in large bookstores. The Victorian attitude that sex was naughty makes this a surprising turn-on.

13. *Illusions of a Lady.* An X-rated film that has become something of a classic and is now out on a video cassette. It has more touches of artistry than most such films, with an interesting score and attractive costumes and even a vestige of a plot line—rare among X-rated films.

14. *Turn On: With the World's Most Sensuous Music.* An album (also available on cassette) of ten romantic selections from classical music. It includes, of course, Ravel's *Bolero* as well as excerpts from *Romeo and Juliet, Tristan and Isolde,* and several piano concertos.

15. Any of the *Black Cat* paperbacks. These books are published by Grove Press and generally priced under four dollars. Most of the authors are anonymous, but the writing is definitely better than the average pornographic book. Some current titles are *Birch in the Boudoir; Davina, or the Romance of Mesmerism; Darling;* and *Crimson Hairs: An Erotic Mystery.*

16. *Solitudes.* A series of albums (also on cassette) that recreates the sounds of very romantic natural settings. One album is recorded on a still northern lake; another features the ocean surf on sand and rocks; a third is a roaring waterfall; there's also dawn on the desert and a spring morning on the prairie. These are wonderful backgrounds for your own private fantasies!

17. *Victoria's Secret* catalog. The sexiest underwear—teddies, G-strings, garter belts, silk nighties—is photographed on models who are obviously not wearing anything else, in luxurious bedroom settings. The nice part about it is that when he finds something that really turns him on, he can buy it for you.

18. *Tantra: The Yoga of Sex.* This new book by Omar Garrison is accurate and informative; if you can't find it in your bookstore, look for any book on the subject of Tantra Yoga. You and your lover will be torn between amusement and amazement as you read about these esoteric sexual practices and positions.

19. Drawings by Aubrey Beardsley, which are available from several different publishers. The artist's black-and-white drawings and prints are fascinatingly bizarre, very sensual, and just a touch kinky.

20. A recent issue of *Playgirl,* a magazine your lover almost certainly doesn't buy for himself. There's usually a photo-story of seduction that is sure to entertain him, jokes and cartoons you can share—and the provocative suggestion that *you* are turned on by male sexuality!

CHAPTER SEVEN

Touring the
Erogenous Zones

It's a shame that when people think and talk about "sex," they generally mean nothing more than intercourse. The many sex manuals out on the market today concentrate on telling you what part to put where and how to operate it, so as to arrive as quickly as possible at the desired goal of orgasm. All the other pleasurable and sexy things you can do with your partner are lumped together under the heading of "foreplay," with the distinct implication that they are worth mentioning only because they might lead up to the grand event of coitus. What a joyless attitude!

The truth of the matter is that the possibilities for sexual enjoyment are virtually endless— limited only by your time, energy, and imagination. In the right hands, any part of the body can be an erogenous zone. "One of the most intense sexual experiences I've ever had," says Rosemary, "was the night Tim concentrated most of his lovemaking on my feet. He stroked my ankles, he kissed my arches, then he went on to suck my toes, one by one. I don't think it's something I'd like to do every time we make love, but somehow, that night . . . the sensations just drove me crazy!"

Obviously, not everyone would find this sensation erotic (perhaps because there aren't enough Tims around to make it that way). Some people *do* find feet very sexy . . . toes a delicious delicacy (Michael Franks has written a wonderful song in praise of this preference, called "Popsicle Toes") . . . sandals a provocative come-on. Others associate them with smelly socks and wouldn't dream of putting their mouths anywhere near one. Obviously, with each new partner, you have to learn about preferences, fantasies, and physiology, to know what will turn him on. Finding out should not be a taxing assignment.

The mind is capable of much more variety than the body, so it may take a lot of pleasant experimentation to learn exactly what turns on the mind of a particular man. Physical reactions tend to be more similar, and therefore they are easier to predict, even with a new lover. Moreover, nature provides good clues as to which parts of the body are most likely to be sexually responsive. Since physical response of any kind depends on being able to feel the stimulus, the first general principle is that erogenous zones are likely to be areas that are richly endowed with nerve endings. Fingertips and tongues, for example, are parts of the human body that were designed for testing the environment and are therefore densely packed with nerve endings; so it's not surprising that they should be easy to stimulate sexually as well. On the other hand, the skin around the elbow has very few nerve endings (you may have learned as a child that no matter how hard you pinch that fold of skin, you still can't feel it). Therefore, even the most ardent and skillful licking and sucking there is unlikely to arouse any response.

Sexual arousal is closely linked to tension; it is, in fact, a process of building up tension for an eventual explosive relief. This provides another clue to likely spots for erogenous zones. Areas of the body that are ticklish—under the arms, the sides of the waist, the bottoms of the feet—may also be susceptible to the kind of tension that results in erotic stimulation.

Please touch . . . everywhere

The skin is really a giant erogenous zone. It is an important organ of communication with the outside world, and much of that communication has an emotional component. For example, studies show that infants need constant touches on the skin to grow and thrive and develop normally; sick people get well faster with the aid of the human touch; stroking the skin relaxes and soothes the emotionally disturbed. So it's not surprising to learn that touching the skin is also a very effective sexual stimulant.

When you are in love with someone, just brushing his arm with yours has all the impact of an electric shock. But even without the magnifying effects of love, touching a man can be a gratifying experience for both of you. Even through the barrier of layers of heavy clothing, the mere warmth of the contact can strike a spark. And on bare skin, one touch is worth a thousand words.

When you want to touch, the best motion is a firm, but gentle, unhesitant stroke with the fingertips. Apply it rhythmically to his back, his chest, his legs, his shoulders, his forearms. Check to see how he responds when you switch from using your fingertips to using your nails; draw them lightly, gently, over his skin. You can alternate between up-and-down strokes and lazy circles; the important thing is not to do anything too hurriedly, and not to switch from one motion to another too quickly or too frequently. Sensuality is closely associated with relaxation, and although your partner will appreciate variety, you should spare him genuine surprises.

And remember that your ability to touch his skin is not limited to the use of your fingers. Touch him with your mouth, your tongue, even your teeth. Plant a row of kisses down his side, nibble the back of his neck, lick the inside of his upper arm, or his underarm (this is a proven turn-on). You can also touch him with your eyelashes, in fluttering butterfly kisses, your cheeks, your nose. Women with long hair may use it like a soft brush. Don't be afraid to try it every way.

Your touch will probably be appreciated everywhere, but some areas are likely to be more responsive than others.

Hands and Feet

Hands can definitely be sex objects! By all means, stroke them and kiss them. Lick the skin on the palms and the back of the hands. Kissing, nibbling, and especially sucking a man's fingers can be an amazingly erotic activity, emphasizing their phallic aspect. Toes are also sensitive and many men enjoy having their feet rubbed or stroked . . . or even kissed—an act that has a symbolic quality of a very different nature.

Eyes and Ears

Eyelids are a very sensitive area (think of how strongly you feel even a stray eyelash) and many men respond immediately when you softly kiss their closed eyelids, or lick them, or even blow gently over them. The erotic potential of ears may be more familiar to you. In addition to the usual kissing and licking, there's the never-fail "blow in my ear and I'll follow you anywhere" or a gentle tug with your lips on his earlobe. Another sexy little game is to point your tongue and gently insert the tip into his ear in a slow back-and-forth motion; this activity is stimulating not only for the physical sensations aroused in his ear but also because of the mental effect of the obvious imagery of penetration.

Navel and Abdomen

The skin on the abdomen is also very sensitive. It's a prime target for stroking, and most men prefer a very firm pressure as you get nearer the groin. Licking and sucking are also likely to arouse him. He may respond favorably to the feeling of your fingers running through the hair that grows in this area, or the more forceful stimulus of a gentle tug. The navel is a focus of special sensitivity. Try kissing it, licking it, even inserting your tongue in a probing motion that mimics the movements of intercourse.

Nipples

Male nipples, although they are not functional, are constructed very much like the female version, and thus they are just as likely to be a source of pleasure in lovemaking. You can stroke his nipples lightly with your fingertips, lick them, suck them, even bite them tenderly, just as he does yours. Most men will signal their physical response to this treatment the same way you do, in an involuntary tightening and erection of the nipples. A difference to bear in mind is that although many women may continue to enjoy attention to their nipples throughout the entire course of lovemaking, men, as a general rule, prefer it to be a preliminary.

Inside of the Thighs

The skin inside the thighs, from just above the knees on up to the groin area, is happily responsive to a light touch, an affectionate lick, and also to a firmer pressure and a kneading motion. Tantalize him by taking care to avoid even accidental contact with the genitals when you begin, but eventually, those long strokes inside the thighs can extend all the way up to include the eagerly waiting scrotum and penis.

Buttocks

Men's buttocks seem to be the current "in" erogenous zone; there has been a sudden spate of books and calendars extolling the sexy appeal of that area. Although this craze may be somewhat overdone, it is good to remind yourself that the male derriere has all the sexual potential of the female variety. Touching it can certainly turn *you* on (since we human beings almost never expose our bottoms to drying sunlight and harsh wind, the skin there is generally soft, smooth, and eminently touchable in both sexes), and it will also do the same for him. Stroke the buttocks gently, knead them, or lick and bite— all of these are pleasant sensations for the recipient. As a general rule, you can assume that anything that feels good when it is done to your buttocks will arouse the same feelings in him when you reciprocate.

Anus

In many important physiological ways, the anus is closely related to the genitals. It is connected to the same nerves, it is covered by the same type of "sexual skin," and it often contracts the same way during orgasm. The male anatomy adds even more potential for arousal because both the base of the penis and the small oval prostate gland are located nearby, and they are sensitive to even the slightest feeling of pressure. However, for psychological reasons, many people find it impossible to regard the anus as a source of sexual pleasure and one or the other partner may find the idea distasteful. If both of you *are* willing (and you may be more so if a shared bath or shower beforehand has assured you of your partner's cleanliness), he will derive great stimulation from a slow soft rubbing of the surface of the anus—and the skin between the anus and the base of the scrotum—along with kissing and licking. Slide the tip of a finger slowly inside the anus and continue the gentle massage, with just a bit of extra pressure directed toward the base of the penis. Many men find this intensely erotic, and they may like to have it continued throughout the various stages of your lovemaking.

Scrotum and Testicles

The scrotum, or the skin covering the testicles, is extremely sensitive. A man will feel the lightest touch, or you can blow softly, or use the mouth and tongue. Some men like a sucking sensation and even enjoy having you take a testicle gently into your mouth. One common complaint heard from men is that most women are *too* gentle and too tentative in handling the testicles. Perhaps it's because women recognize it as an area of vulnerability—and certainly a vicious squeeze or direct attack would be painful. But that part of the body is not really so delicate, and the chances are good that your partner would appreciate a little added pressure in your touch.

Penis

For most men, this is the primary site of sexual stimulation. The very tip of the head of the penis is generally the most sensitive spot, and many enjoy having it rubbed, licked, and kissed. Just under the head is a little fold of skin, another area of extreme sensitivity. The shaft of the penis is constructed to be responsive to pressure, so unless you have a very talented mouth, your hands are likely to give him more enjoyment. Some men like the feeling of encircling pressure at the base of the penis, whereas others find it painful; try a gentle pressure at first and judge his response. You will find further suggestions in Chapter Ten, in the section on oral sex; meanwhile, bear in mind this comment from one of the wisest sex therapists today, Dr. Avodah K. Offit in her book, *Night Thoughts*: "Treating a man's penis not only as a beloved aspect of his body but also as a unique being, like an infant or bird, requiring the most nurturant and elegant care, is a major secret of mutual gratification."

CHAPTER EIGHT

Your Enjoyment Is His Greatest Turn-on

"Was it good for you?"

That question, whether actually spoken or only wondered about, hangs in the air every time you make love. Our cultural attitudes make men more responsible for sexual success than women. The man is supposed to initiate sex, to orchestrate the entire process, and to cap the performance by "giving" the woman an orgasm. It's a heavy demand, so it is not really surprising that most men are very anxious to find out how well they have performed. In fact, that performance anxiety may even surface early in the encounter and interfere with his ability to "make it good," either for you or himself.

One thing you can do to prevent the chilling effects of performance anxiety is to learn to *share* the responsibility for lovemaking with your man. The more you can make it clear to him that you genuinely view sex as a joint activity (rather than something he "does" to you) and yourself as a full partner in the process, the freer he will feel—and therefore the more he will be able to give you.

Another thing you can do is learn to communicate with your partner about how you feel during the time you are making love. He'll certainly appreciate it if you let him know afterward that you enjoyed it, but he'll appreciate it even more if you let him in on that fact *during* your lovemaking. It will put his mind at ease, and, better yet, it will definitely turn him on even more.

Talking about sex

Many women find it extremely difficult to talk to their lovers about sex; it's another one of those things our mothers told us not to do. We're afraid he'll misunderstand, conclude that we are sex-crazed, or too coldly analytical, or dirty-minded, or naive—or all of the above! Particularly, we hesitate to tell him just what he would most like to hear: that we are really enjoying sex, when he likes to hear it, *during* sex.

It is definitely *true* that many men like to hear a woman "talk dirty" while they are making love; there are probably many more willing listeners than there are talkers. But what if you're not comfortable talking like a quote from the latest Harold Robbins novel? What do you say? Well, "The earth moved," is certainly too corny.

To say, "Oh, it's as big as a baseball bat!" would in most cases be obviously insincere. To beg, "Quick, thrust your throbbing organ of steel deep inside my quivering womb" would probably cause both of you intense embarrassment.

The simple approach is easiest and best. All you want to do is reassure him that you are a full partner in the process of mutual enjoyment. Try one of these:

"Oh, that feels good."

"That's nice."

"I like what you're doing."

"You're wonderful."

"You're turning me on."

More specific praise can be fine too, as long as it's truthful (or close enough to truthful to pass for sincere). An obvious exaggeration about his size or staying power or masterful technique may sound more false than appreciative. And comparisons, even when they're intended to be flattering, may leave him uneasy. Shelly tells a story about the first time she and her boyfriend made love. "Afterward, I told him extravagantly, 'You're the best lover I've ever had.' He shot back quickly, 'Just how big is your sample?' *That* certainly put me on the spot! I realized that what I had meant as a compliment made him feel demeaned, as if he was just another name on my list."

One thing that many women *have* learned to say when they are making love is "I love you." That's fine if it's true, and will make both of you feel closer and more intimate. *But don't say it if it isn't true*. Don't say it because you think he wants to hear it. Don't say it because you expect it out of yourself. Don't say it because you want it to become true, and don't say it because you want him to say the same thing back to you! The feeling of real love means too much to be devalued for any of those reasons. It's easy enough to find some other way to say what you really mean, which may be simply that you like his company or that you have enjoyed him as a sexual partner. "I like being with you," or "It was a very special evening," or "You really are a nice man" are good examples of the kind of response that is warm and friendly and reassuring—and honest.

Actions speak louder than words

It's nice to be able to put your enjoyment into words, but remember that not all your responses have to be verbal. You can also *show* him that you are turned on and that you like the things that are happening between you. For many women, this is even harder than saying it, but it is something which when you've learned to do it, can be particularly rewarding. If you've established an atmosphere of mutual trust and respect with your partner, then you should feel free to be open about your sexual responses.

Let him hear your breathing quicken as you feel more and more aroused. Let him feel your bottom wiggle, your pelvis move, as his touches and caresses cause your excitement to deepen. Snuggle up to him spontaneously at any time during sex to show your affection. He will be satisfied that he is an effective lover, and your responses will encourage his own, thus creating a lovely spiral of gratification.

"After Rob and I had been lovers for about a month," reminisces Lisa, "we had an unusually long and intense session of lovemaking when I returned from a short business trip. Before, it had always seemed important to me to keep myself under control; I didn't like the idea of acting like the star of a porno film, thrashing around and screaming at the top of my voice. But this particular time I was so excited, that, when I finally came, I did cry out, and also I grabbed his shoulder and clutched tight, regardless of the damage my nails might do." Lisa giggles. "Afterward, I felt so embarrassed about my behavior, and I was lying there anxiously trying to think of some acceptable way to explain it to Rob. But before I got up my courage, he leaned over, gave me a big kiss on the cheek, and said, 'You really enjoyed yourself that time, didn't you?' I nodded and he went on, 'Hearing you enjoy yourself makes it more exciting for me too.' Since then, with Rob's encouragement, I have gotten much better at letting him share my excitement, and it's better for both of us. I guess my old attitude was just one more way of saying *nice girls don't,* but I'm glad I found out that they do."

Lisa is absolutely right. Nice girls *do* moan and make noises and move their bodies appreciatively. And nice men like it. It's also perfectly okay to bite and scratch . . . although of course it's not a good idea to inflict serious pain or lasting damage. But many men wear their love scratches and bites like honorable scars from the battle of love; in fact, they may even actively fantasize about receiving them!

The "message" of orgasm

In the bad old days, if we are to believe the historians, men didn't even know women could have orgasms. And even after they found out, they still didn't care whether it happened or not; sex was really considered to be a man's pleasure and a woman's obligation. But in the last several decades, there has been a heavy stress on the subject of the woman's pleasure in general and the female orgasm in particular. The result is that it has somehow become a symbol of *male* achievement. The woman's orgasm is the final seal of approval on his prowess as a lover, his guarantee that it was indeed good for her. Well, it's nice that he's concerned, but sometimes a man's stubborn determination to prove he can bring a woman to climax turns into a prolonged and somewhat disagreeable struggle.

It's undeniably true that an orgasm can be a delight not only for you but for your partner as well. And sometimes the physical stimulation from your orgasmic contractions adds enough to the mental stimulation that comes from his sense of having contributed to that pleasure to set off an orgasm in your partner. He will appreciate your acknowledgment that your climax is truly a joint achievement, so by all means, if you do have one, let him know about it. Tell him in words, or let him know by your actions, or, most intimate of all, let him *feel* for himself, by helping him to recognize the sensation of your orgasmic contractions. Your pleasure will turn him on. Since many men try to control their own sexual responses until they have satisfied their partner, it may also signal him to actively pursue his own climax.

But what if you *don't* have an orgasm? If you think there's some way to change the situation, you will be doing both of you a favor by finding a way to let him know. But sometimes, it doesn't matter what he does or how he does it; you recognize that you are simply not going to reach a climax. The sensations are nice, but it's not going anywhere. You may find that perfectly acceptable, but trouble often begins when your partner doesn't. Many men will take your lack of orgasm as a message, the significance of which is their own failure. The man becomes more and more determined to "succeed" and that makes you feel under more and more pressure. The outcome of this situation is easy to predict: the harder he tries, the less you are able to enjoy it, and that's not good for either of you. As one woman put it, "I feel like some accident victim who is failing to respond to resuscitation, and I just want to tell him, 'Please, no extraordinary measures!'"

It's unfortunate that so many people think of orgasm as the only goal of sexual activity, because it so often isn't. Many women have told me that it's the closeness and intimacy of mutual affection that provides their real gratification. How can you change your lover's attitude, so he can relax and enjoy making love without worrying about the final goal?

One way some women choose is simply to fake a climax. The pluses they list are that you have sent him the message he wanted to receive— that you find him a good lover—and you have eliminated a source of looming tension. With a new lover, or one who is for some reason feeling insecure, this might be an acceptable choice. But it has some real drawbacks. Your dishonesty may diminish the sense of sharing that makes any relationship, including a purely sexual one, work. You may feel resentful at what you see as being forced into this stratagem. You may find that you have signaled an end to further sexual stimulation which might have been very pleasant for you even though it didn't lead to orgasm. And you may find yourself faking orgasms throughout the rest of your relationship!

An alternate approach, and one that seems particularly appropriate with a lover with whom you share emotional and psychological intimacy as well as sex, is to help your partner understand that your enjoyment of sexual activity is not limited to orgasm. Orgasm in the male is essential if you want to start a family, but otherwise it is just one aspect of the pleasure that comes from making love. Others are caressing, closeness, giving him pleasure, mutual enjoyment. He will find it easier to accept if you give him the message he sought from your orgasm in other ways. Tell him he is a wonderful lover, show him that you are responding to his caresses. Your reassurance should remove the pressure generated by the situation and allow both of you to relax and enjoy the pleasant sensations of the moment.

Remember, there is a person attached to that thing

With practice, you can learn to communicate your appreciation of your partner as a sexual being, and that will help him take even more pleasure in your lovemaking. But don't concentrate so totally on his role as a lover that you ignore his other human aspects. Everyone likes to be sexy, but no one wants to be *only* a sex object. Make sure that you acknowledge your respect for him as a whole person. Tell him you like his thoughtfulness or that you appreciate his generosity of spirit. Slip a pillow under his head to make him a bit more comfortable. Give him a chaste kiss on the forehead or an affectionate pat on the arm. Let him know that you see him as a complete person, with whom you happen to be sharing the wonderful experience of making love.

CHAPTER NINE

Sexual Intercourse

The importance of honest communication about sex

"At one point, I nearly ended my relationship with Peggy," said Jason. "I liked her, I respected her, but in bed . . . well, frankly, I became just plain bored. By about the third time we slept together, we had fallen into an unchanging routine of lovemaking. After dinner, on the living-room sofa, I would kiss her and caress her breasts. Then we marched off to the bedroom, where I stroked her until she became aroused. She'd reciprocate with a few minutes of oral sex. When that really started to excite me, we would move immediately to have intercourse, with me on top pumping away. I'd always try to control myself until I was sure she'd had her climax, and then I'd let myself go, so my own would come a minute or two later. Afterward, she would cuddle in my arms until we both fell asleep.

"It never changed, not one time. She never

suggested anything different, she never surprised me with a new move. And I felt she expected me to behave with the same predictability: it seemed like the height of bad manners and poor taste to initiate any changes in this ritual. A few months of such monotony made me lose interest in making love to her . . . it was like we were playing the same videotape over and over and over."

Peggy smiled. "The sad thing is that I felt exactly the same way he did. I was afraid I would offend him, or cause him to lower his opinion of me if I made any suggestions about changing this routine, so I just tried to endure it because of my affection for Jason. But I'd gotten to the point where the only way I could enjoy sex was to fantasize that Jason was someone else. I knew we were in trouble."

For Peggy and Jason, the solution came as the result of an accident. He slipped and fell on the icy steps of a friend's house, and the resulting wrench of his back made it impossible for him to make love in the usual missionary position for some weeks. That handicap broke their pattern. They replaced it with new activities: they had intercourse with Peggy on top, or they took turns giving and receiving oral sex. Each discovered that the other loved the change in their dull routine, so as soon as Jason's back was better, they happily launched themselves on months of erotic experimentation. Now their relationship is better than ever.

But the unfortunate part about this story is that it took an accident to bring about the change that both partners had wanted all along in their sex life. How much better it would be to communicate such feelings directly! In the previous chapter, we talked about how you can learn to send your partner both verbal and nonverbal messages about your satisfaction with the way he makes you feel. You can use much the same techniques to send him messages about what you'd *like* him to do. For this purpose, nonverbal suggestions can sometimes be very effective. For example, you can draw his head down to your breast, or gently place his hand on your vaginal lips. He'll get the idea, yet he's still free to choose exactly how to follow it up.

But sometimes nonverbal suggestions simply aren't specific enough, or they are too hard for your partner to interpret. For example, if you pull your breast slowly away from his mouth, what does it mean? Are you finding the sensation disagreeable because he is sucking too hard? Are you so excited you want him to let up for a moment? Or are you simply ready to go on to something else? Or do you want to stop making love altogether? These are things you are going to have to put in words if you want to be understood clearly.

When you switch to verbal communication, there are some things you should try to remember. One is to refrain from making too many requests or suggestions at the same time:

you don't want your partner to feel that you are barking out orders for him to follow. The other important point is to phrase your suggestions in a *positive* way. Don't *blame:* "I don't know why you keep doing that when you know I don't like it." Don't *criticize:* "That isn't working and I want you to stop." Instead, tell him, "I feel in the mood for . . ." or "You've made me feel so good I'd just like to lie here quietly with you for a few minutes," or "I'm really enjoying this and there's something else I'd enjoy too." As long as you don't make your partner feel he is being judged and then attacked for some failure, he will probably be very happy to find out what you want— and happy to do it for you.

But what about getting him to tell you what *he* wants? That can be a much more difficult problem. A man who can be downright brazen when he approaches you may turn out to be quite shy when it comes to revealing his own preferences and responses. Another complication is that many men have been brainwashed by the sexual myth that depicts the Real Man as ever-eager, ready to screw anything that moves, able to stand erect at the slightest stimulus. They don't like to admit even to themselves that they may not respond to certain situations or some kinds of caresses, and they are even less likely to reveal it to you. For much the same reasons, many men have never stopped to ask themselves what they really *do* like; they are too intent on "doing it" and on proving to their partners that they are good lovers to take the time to notice their own reactions. One of the nicest things you can do for your lover is help him discover these reactions. You may be able to open up a whole new dimension of sexual satisfaction in his life.

How do you teach him to talk?

Encourage him to put his preferences, his reactions, into words. You might start with questions he can answer with a simple yes or no.

"Am I stroking you hard enough?"

"Is it better like this?"

"Is that comfortable for you?"

"Would you like to turn over?"

Once he is comfortable with that sort of verbalization, you can move on to more open-ended questions.

"What can I do next to make you feel good?"

"Which way do you like it best?"

"What would you enjoy doing next?"

"What would you like to teach me?"

Once you start encouraging your partner to express himself, remember that you have incurred a responsibility in regard to your own response. If you have asked him what he wants, it is unfair (and definitely counterproductive) to react by criticizing his preferences. You may face problems when he tells you he wants to do something you find distasteful. For example, one of my close friends told me about a lover who finally opened up to reveal his desire for her to urinate in his mouth while he was giving her oral sex; she found the idea disturbing. But she handled the situation with her usual tact. She refrained from blurting out, "Oh, that's too kinky!" or any other negative judgment. Instead she simply told him that she would feel uncomfortable doing it, and then apologized for not being able to manage it. Since she continued to treat him with unchanged respect and affection, they soon found other activities that led to mutual gratification.

Some men find it easier to talk about sex when they are not in the middle of doing it. Your partner may respond more openly if you bring up the subject over dinner, or while you're reading the Sunday paper. Or try discussing it over the phone. Many researchers have discovered that interviewees will talk much more freely over the phone than they will face-to-face, and the principle is just as true for this type of conversation. Another possibility is to make the conversation indirect. Ask him to tell you about a favorite fantasy, or a recent dream about sex, or the most erotic story he ever heard from one of his friends; the chances are good that he will reveal what he really wants.

His body can tell you what he likes

Even if he resists your invitations to tell you about his preferences during lovemaking, you can find them out in other ways. A good lover is a good detective, looking for clues to her partner's response. Only experience can teach you how your particular man reacts, but you might start by looking for some of these physical signs that in most men accompany increasing levels of sexual arousal after the initial erection:

- Faster, noiser breathing.
- A slight flush, especially on the chest and legs.
- Increased muscular tension in the legs and stomach, which may be manifested by stretching and flexing, and even occasionally a cramp.
- Erect nipples.
- Swollen earlobes (yes, really!).
- A thickening of the skin covering the testicles.
- Movement of the testicles up toward the body; they may feel "tight" when you touch them.
- Enlargement of the urethra, the tube (it looks like a vein) that runs the length of the shaft on the underside of the penis, through which the semen will soon travel.
- Reddening of the head of the penis.
- More vigorous, perhaps involuntary, pelvic thrusting.

In addition to these common physiological responses, most men (and women too) develop a pattern of behavior associated with increased arousal that you can learn to recognize. For example, your lover may make particular types of noises; he may wrap his arms around you more tightly; he may suddenly look deep into your eyes; he may abruptly change the rhythm of his movements. The more you learn about his habitual "choreography," the easier it will be to adjust your own actions to give him the most pleasure.

The height of pleasure: the male orgasm

Although not all sexual pleasure requires the participation of an erect penis, the act of intercourse certainly does. In most men, ejaculation of semen is followed soon afterward by loss of erection, and except in very young (or very rare) men, it may be an hour or more before a second erection is possible. So in most cases, the act of ejaculation by the male signals the end of sexual intercourse.

An interesting question, currently the focus of much research, is whether ejaculation and male orgasm are one and the same event. Although most people (including medical doctors like Masters and Johnson, in their pioneering work on the physiology of human sexual response) label the moment of ejaculation as the peak of the male climax, there is, in fact, increasing evidence that men can achieve a sudden peak of high sexual excitement, with the usual rapid increase in respiration, blood pressure, and heartbeat—in other words, an orgasm—*without* any accompanying ejaculation. Men may therefore be as multi-orgasmic as women; it's just that neither they nor we understood that these multiple peaks of excitement were indeed orgasms. And since most men are in the habit of ejaculating at the time of their first peak, they remain unaware of their ability to achieve more than one.

If there truly is a difference between orgasm and ejaculation, then you can help your partner learn to enjoy more than one orgasm. (And even if one is all he has, you've still extended the period of his enjoyment.) The secret, obviously, lies in his voluntary control of the complicated process of ejaculation. Some men are already quite skilled at this, sometimes so skilled that they don't even realize they are doing it, and all they need is your willing cooperation when they exercise it. When your partner suddenly slows or stops his thrusting motion, or stiffens into momentary immobility, or even withdraws briefly, it is usually because he is concentrating on the avoidance of ejaculation. The most helpful thing you can do is behave in a similar manner, and slow or stop your own movements. This is definitely a point in the process of lovemaking when he should remain in control of the situation.

But not all men know how voluntarily to avoid arriving at the point of ejaculation. The first thing you can do is make him aware of your willingness to participate in his learning process. Be aware that he may jump to the conclusion that you have brought the subject up because you are disappointed in his performance. So bring the subject up tactfully, with a positive statement that this is something you want to do for him. For example: "You make me feel so good that I want to make sure I am giving you a lot in return." Or: "Maybe you'd enjoy being able to go on a little longer."

With your encouragement and support, your partner can start to discover what works for him. (As with all sexual responses, not everyone works the same way.) Here are some of the ways a man can control his ejaculation: He may:

- Change the rhythm of his pelvic thrusts— usually from fast to slow.
- After the depth of his thrusts, to avoid deep penetration and its stimulating feeling of pressure.
- Switch from an in-and-out motion of the penis to a slow rotating movement.
- Consciously relax the muscles in his genital area. This may require him to practice beforehand to locate the key muscle (called the bulbocavernosus) and to experience and identify the sensation of contracting and relaxing. The best

way to do this is to imagine urinating and then cutting off the stream and then releasing it again. The relaxation that released the urine is the action he should try during lovemaking.

• Attempt to urinate. The tube through which semen is ejaculated, the urethra, is also the tube through which urine is released. A set of valves controls this switch, and therefore the process of urination blocks ejaculation. The sensation of trying to urinate will often close the valve and prevent ejaculation.

There is a technique, originally developed by Masters and Johnson in their pioneering treatment of men who suffer from premature ejaculation, that you can use to help your partner prevent ejaculation. It is called the penile squeeze, and it can only be employed with the full cooperation of both partners. When he senses that he is about to come, he tells you, and you apply the squeeze. Encircle the base of the penis with your thumb and forefinger and gently squeeze at the same time that you press your hand toward his body. This technique is completely reliable, but subsequent research has indicated that for most men it is unnecessarily complicated. You can generally accomplish the same goal simply by stopping all motion and excitation. You and your partner simply agree on a signal—he says "stop" or he squeezes your hand—and you both stop immediately until his excitement has subsided and he is ready to resume making love. Use this technique to help your lover improve his voluntary control of ejaculation. If he has a serious problem, he should work it out with a therapist, either on his own or with you; trying to administer therapy on your own may quickly become too emotionally burdensome for both of you and it can cause the end of your relationship.

One other way you can help your partner enjoy himself more during lovemaking is to encourage him to experience that final moment, whenever it comes, to the fullest. Sex therapists have learned that most men can enhance their orgasms by a variety of accompanying actions that heighten the feeling of released tension. One such action is the *contraction* of the bulbocavernosus, the muscle that he learned to relax in order to delay ejaculation; tightening that muscle may increase the force of ejaculation and therefore his own sensations. Another orgasm-enhancing action is, oddly enough, breathing. It seems that many men tense up just before ejaculation and unconsciously hold their breath. Rapid deep breathing, even panting, can increase your partner's pleasure.

In general, men seem to be afraid that they might offend their partner if they act too "bestial" at the moment of climax. So they restrain themselves from excessive body movements, cries and groans, biting and sucking. But for many men (and women as well) such actions exaggerate the feeling of release, both physically and emotionally, and therefore they stimulate more satisfying, often longer-lasting, orgasms. So encourage your lover to feel free to do whatever feels good. Tell him how good it is for you to know that his being with you can make him feel so good, that you want to share the moment with him, that you find his excitement sexy and stimulating and rewarding. And you'll find that you have spoken the absolute truth!

Positions . . . and their advantages

Some sex manuals put heavy stress on the importance of choosing the "best" position for sex. They recommend positions for pregnant women, for men with heart conditions, for people who are overweight or underweight, for the tall and the short, for the man who wants deep penetration and the woman who needs heavy clitoral stimulation . . . it's a wonder they don't have something special for accountants or Aquarians!

How many positions are there? The book *Man's Body* illustrates 153. (The mere thought of trying to make love 153 different ways is exhausting.) But on closer examination, it seems that most of these positions are merely small variations. For example, your partner can switch from leaning on his hands to his elbows; you can put both feet on the bed or lift one leg in the air. In actual fact, there are no more than eight or ten major variations.

Obviously, it can get boring to make love in exactly the same position every time; and it is generally the case that men get bored more easily than women. On the other hand, you may find that some positions simply don't work for you, either because they don't provide one or the other of you with some important type of stimulation, or because one (or both) of you is not physically comfortable, or because you have some negative emotional response to the situation. Don't feel that you and your partner have to turn into sexual acrobats, but do at least experiment with introducing some variety of positions into your repertoire. You may discover something that turns both of you on.

Here is a brief list of the major variations.

1. Man on Top

Some men like this, the most common position, because they can be in complete control of the thrusting movements of intercourse (and therefore of their ejaculation). Another reason for its popularity is that it allows maximum body contact between the partners; your lover really can feel that you are touching him all over. For most couples, this position permits both mouth-to-mouth and mouth-to-breast contact, but if your lover is markedly taller or shorter than you, he may not be able to reach both without moving up or down. Your own position can vary from being stretched out full length to having both legs in the air and your buttocks raised off the bed. (A pillow or two under your derriere will accomplish much the same effect, without the resulting strain on your muscles.) In general, the higher you raise your legs, the deeper your lover can penetrate, which some men find more stimulating.

2. Woman on Top, Sitting

All the woman-on-top positions give your lover the chance to relax and let someone else do the work (although if he wants to, he can of course still thrust upward). Many men find it a real turn-on to have the woman in control of the frequency and depth of thrusting, since it relieves them of their customary burden of responsibility. When you are sitting upright (or squatting or kneeling over him), your lover will be able to watch your excitement, which will feed his own, and he will be able to give you additional stimulation by touching your breasts and genital area. Some men assert that they feel a lapping or sucking sensation on their penises in this position.

3. Woman on Top, Lying Down

If you lie down on top of your lover, rather than sitting, you can give him the advantage of mouth-to-mouth contact, or let him fondle your breasts, and some couples find that this increases their feeling of emotional intimacy. However, this position does decrease the depth of penetration. A variation is to lie down so you are facing his feet rather than his head. This permits him to stroke and stimulate your buttocks, but it loses most of the feeling of intimacy.

4. Sitting, Face-to-Face

This is a playful position, perhaps because it's so much like sitting on his lap, and one again that puts the woman in control of most of the movement. Although you can manage it while you are sitting on the floor, with the man supporting his weight on his hands, it will be much more comfortable for both of you to find a nice big upholstered chair (and that will leave his hands free for better things). It permits lots of eye contact and kissing, which are important to many couples. And it's very handy when you are for some reason confined to a small space: one man told me this is the way he and his girlfriend make love on a transcontinental flight—locked into the bathroom!

5. Side by Side

This is one of the most relaxing of all positions, and it also permits the greatest mutuality, since the motion of thrusting is equally easy for the man and the woman: you can take turns being the active partner. If you like, your heads can be close enough together for kissing—but remember that the farther *apart* your heads are, the deeper his penetration will be. This position is a good choice for those occasions when your lovemaking goes on for a long time, since it doesn't require supporting either your own or your partner's weight.

6. Rear Entry, Kneeling

In this position, the man is kneeling behind you while you are on all fours. The disadvantage is that you can't see one another's faces and he often can't reach your breasts. This position is often called "doggy style" and that similarity makes some women uncomfortable in assuming it. But many men find the sight of their partner's buttocks extremely erotic, and they also enjoy the chance to stroke and fondle them—and that can turn the woman on.

7. Rear Entry, Sitting

Another way to achieve rear entry is for the man to sit down and then the woman to sit on top, like two stacked chairs in an auditorium.

Like all woman-on-top positions, this gives you the chance to initiate more of the movement during intercourse and can therefore be very relaxing, even nurturing, for your lover. Although there is the disadvantage that you are not facing one another, he can caress your breasts. Some women adore rear entry positions because there is a lot of stimulation to the sensitive skin between the vagina and the anus; and many men like it because the angle of entry into the vagina creates an exciting pressure on the shaft of the penis.

8. The Wheelbarrow

Some couples insist this position permits the very closest contact between penis and vagina. Your lover stands near the edge of a high bed or a table of the correct height; you lie down in front of him and wrap your legs around his waist or shoulders. This does require that both of you be in fairly fit condition, since you must do what amounts to an extended leg lift and he must support the weight of your lower body. Still, as long as you don't try to stay in the position too long, it permits very deep penetration, full genital contact, and a lot of excitement.

Whichever position you and your lover choose, don't worry about the "instructions." There is no right way or wrong way to make love, so just relax and let yourself feel all the sensations.

Make adjustments for your particular situation, for each person's specific size and shape and physiology and emotional needs. You are two unique people who create between you a special moment.

CHAPTER TEN

Other Sexual Pleasures

"If you want to give your readers some really good advice," said a Chicago businessman, "tell them that sex doesn't begin and end with a penis in a vagina." "That's right," added his friend Max. "Sometimes I decide to keep quiet about what I really like because I'm afraid my girlfriend will respond with distaste, or even downright hostility. The one time I tried to tell her I was interested in experimenting with anal sex, she burst into tears and then got dressed and left my apartment! It took days to get our relationship back on an even keel. To her, the very suggestion meant I didn't respect her."

These men are speaking frankly about a feeling that many other men tell me they share. They would like to experience different sexual activities. But frequently their partners are upset by their requests, and either unwilling or unable to comply with them. So the men are a little dissatisfied, and the women are a little hostile . . . and everybody loses.

If any of the sexual practices discussed in this

chapter really offends you, don't force yourself to try it. Sexual enjoyment requires a healthy dose of relaxation, and also trust, both of which will elude you if you are merely gritting your teeth to try to get through something you consider nasty. Neither of you will get any pleasure from the experience, and there may later be serious repercussions, in the form of anger (yours or his) about the situation and reduced response (again, for either or both of you) to future sexual encounters. However, some women cut off discussion about the subject or hesitate to agree because they aren't sure what will be expected of them, or because they've never tried it and don't know whether they will like it, or because they read or heard something that made it sound disgusting even though they have no firsthand knowledge. If you want to please your partner— and thereby, of course, benefit yourself—don't let any of these attitudes stand in the way of trying something new. See if you like it; if you don't, at least you will know in the future what you are refusing.

When you *do* decide to try something new, remember that you don't have to become an instant expert. Tell your partner frankly, "It's my first time and I'm not sure if I know exactly what to do." Most men will be so delighted by your willingness that they will be especially appreciative of your efforts, however they turn out. And they are also likely to be secretly flattered by assuming the role of teacher in such matters.

Manual stimulation

We generally think of this practice as part of the foreplay that eventually leads to intercourse, but there is no reason that it always has to be the understudy rather than the star. Your lover may sometimes prefer to spend a substantial amount of time enjoying the sensations of your hands stimulating his penis or his testicles, and occasionally he may even want to have his climax that way. (He can then reciprocate by giving you manual stimulation or oral sex until you reach your own climax.)

A little practice can make you very good with your hands. Caress the head of the penis lightly with your fingertips, paying special attention to the sensitive area on the underside. Then grasp the shaft firmly and slide your hand up and down to create a pleasing friction. (It's possible that the friction of a dry hand may in fact be too irritating, so you might try using a little hand lotion, massage oil, or K-Y jelly.) Vary your stroke, as well as its speed: try a circular motion, or apply it to just the head, or just the shaft. Don't forget to add light strokes or gentle scratches on the scrotum and the skin just behind it, as well as the anus if the idea doesn't turn you off. Since you have two hands, you can create several different kinds of stimulation at the same time.

Mutual masturbation

Not too many years ago, masturbation was considered a serious moral lapse, with alarming physical consequences ranging from pimples to idiocy and even hairy palms! None of these threats kept people from masturbating, and research shows that today most men (and women too) begin the practice in their very early teens and may continue it throughout their lives. Perhaps because of the stigma previously attached to masturbation, it is usually considered a form of sexuality somehow inferior to intercourse, and men are often careful to conceal the fact of their occasional masturbation from their sexual partners.

Some therapists take an entirely different, and much more positive, view of masturbation. They suggest that it is really a form of self-acceptance, even self-love; people who don't masturbate to orgasm may be people who can't give themselves permission to enjoy life. There are studies that seem to reinforce this conclusion, suggesting that men and women who masturbate regularly are much less likely to develop serious sexual problems than those who find the idea repugnant.

Our culture tends to identify masturbation as a form of loneliness, something to do when there is no partner available. But some couples find that masturbation makes a pleasant addition to their mutual sexual activities. "I don't see what the big deal is," says one man. "My girlfriend and I are close, we are sharing the experience, the same things happen to my penis that would if she were touching me. It just happens to be my hand instead of hers."

As the speaker indicates, one way to include masturbation in your shared sexual life is for you to watch while he masturbates (some couples find this a good solution to the problem that the man wants more sex than the woman does). He may like the idea that you are really concentrating on his penis—we all have some hidden exhibitionist tendencies—or he may prefer to have you snuggle close to him, kissing and stroking his face, shoulders, and chest to increase the total stimulation. He may enjoy touching you at the same time, or he may revel in the momentary selfishness of having the focus entirely on his own stimulation. There's nothing wrong with this kind of self-centeredness, which we all enjoy, provided he is also willing to reciprocate.

An alternate possibility is that your lover might enjoy watching *you* masturbate. Remember: men are generally very turned on by a woman's excitement, and sometimes they can appreciate it even more if they are not active participants at that moment. Your partner may want to be physically close to you, or he may prefer a bit of distance so he can really see you clearly. This activity is usually a prelude to intercourse, and don't be surprised if your lover's attitude becomes almost competitive, as he strives to give you a better and more exciting experience than you were able to give yourself.

Some couples choose to masturbate simultaneously, either as the main sexual activity, or as another activity *after* an episode of intercourse. Thanks to long familiarity with their own bodies, some men are able to stimulate themselves into a second erection more successfully than you can do it for them. Unfortunately, simultaneous mutual masturbation that is truly enjoyable for both partners is somewhat difficult to achieve. It's hard to concentrate on producing your own pleasure and at the same time be a responsive audience for your partner, and most women find that the result is that they are unable to achieve orgasm. But that's not a serious problem, as long as you explain the situation to your partner and he finds some other way of stimulating you.

Oral Sex

"I remember the first time," says Leslie. "We had been taking a shower together. After he dried off, Mike went into the bedroom. He threw himself down on the bed, stretched luxuriously, and begged like a little boy, 'Eat me! Eat me all up!' I was taken by surprise and I felt very shy, because I'd never done it before. But Mike was so sweet and funny and encouraging that I decided this time I would give it a try. 'Just think of me as your delicious ice-cream cone,' he instructed. 'Hold the cone in your hand . . . like this . . . and now lick the top . . . that's right . . . imagine it's a hot summer day and the ice cream is melting . . . you have to lick harder, faster, to keep it from dripping . . . yes, that's it . . . that's wonderful!' "

As a general rule, men love oral sex. They say it gives incomparable stimulation: the combination of your mouth, tongue, hands, and teeth can create many more sensations than the vagina alone. They also enjoy the feeling of being cared for, catered to, done to instead of doing—in short, being made love to. Some men like it as the preliminary to intercourse, and they prefer not to ejaculate during oral sex. Others may want to climax in oral sex after a period of intercourse in which their partner has her orgasm. Some men make it the second show of a double feature, because they find it much easier to have a second erection and climax with the stimulation of oral sex than they do with vaginal sex. And sometimes they want it to be the one and only act during a session of lovemaking. Any of these patterns is fine, as long as your partner doesn't neglect your satisfaction.

It is undeniable that some women have a distaste for oral sex. They feel they are being used, or they interpret it as the man's wish to avoid contact with the vagina. They may view it as a literal enactment of the domineering statement, "I'm going to shove it down your throat." They think of it as dirty and in particular may feel soiled by the man's ejaculate, so his desire to do that to them seems like a form of attack rather than love.

But men turn out to have a very different set of feelings about oral sex. Many view it as a token of their trust and affection. "After all," comments Max, "I am putting the most vulnerable part of my anatomy into the most dangerous part of hers. Believe me, I wouldn't do that with just anyone." Other men have pointed out that oral sex makes them feel especially close to their partner because she is playing a nurturing role. It is quite common for a man to think of his penis almost as his child (for example, a recent book revealed that Elvis Presley always referred to his penis as "Little Elvis"), so a woman's care of the penis creates a bond that draws the couple close. Other men enjoy the feeling that they are the ones doing the nurturing and giving. "When my girlfriend is sucking my penis," says one, "I feel very tender toward her. During that time, she is the child being suckled, and I am the life giver."

Perhaps if you bear in mind some of the very

positive emotions oral sex may arouse in your partner, you will feel less uncomfortable with the idea. Another way to feel more comfortable is simply to get enough practice to be able to give oral sex skillfully and easily. Many women hesitate not because they really dislike the idea but because they are afraid they will do it "wrong" and give their partner pain instead of pleasure. In fact, the process of giving a man oral sex, called fellatio, is really very easy. All it takes is friendly contact between your mouth and his penis; the subsequent variations are up to you.

What is the best position for oral sex? You will probably feel most comfortable starting out with a position that allows the woman to remain in control of the lovemaking. Your partner might lie on his back, legs apart, while you kneel or crouch between his legs. Another possibility, one that allows a little more affectionate body contact, is to lie down at right angles to your lover, as if you were going to take a nap using his stomach for a pillow; he will be able to stroke your back, and possibly also your buttocks and breasts, at the same time. Some men like to sit on the edge of the bed with their feet on the floor while the woman kneels between his legs; this position also allows the couple to embrace more easily.

Once you feel more confident with oral sex, and trusting of your lover, you might try a "man above" position that permits him to thrust into your mouth; this leaves your hands free to caress his buttocks and anus, increasing his pleasurable sensations. A final possibility, which is most successful for couples who have established good mutual communication, is the position called "69," which allows you to give him oral sex while he does the same for you. You lie on your side, with your head pillowed on one of his thighs between his opened legs, and he lies the same way. Although this does require the ability to concentrate on two things at once—how you are feeling and what you are doing—it can permit a strong sense of sharing and mutuality during oral sex.

If oral sex takes place at the beginning of a lovemaking session, you will want to start with some general stroking of his body, along with kissing, snuggling, and other preliminary activities; he's liable to feel under attack if you simply reach for his crotch (as would you, in his place). After the two of you feel comfortable together, you can begin to work your way, with strokes of the hand and tongue, past his chest, down his stomach and inside his thighs. Then move on to the scrotum, stimulating it too with a combination of kisses and licks, and the anus. By the time you arrive at the penis itself, the chances are good it will be erect and waiting anxiously for your attention. You might first caress the penis lovingly with your hands: every man enjoys the implication that you worship his penis! Then begin to lick the head with your tongue; as always, concentrate on the sensitive underside and work your way down the shaft and back up again.

The next stage, where you take his penis into your mouth, is the one that really gets your partner excited. You can suck gently, move your mouth up and down in a rapid motion, and continue to use your tongue as well. (Think of the motions your tongue makes when you are sucking on a piece of hard candy, and you will make him very happy.) Do remember that your teeth might be surprisingly sharp. Although some men like the sensation of being "scratched" by gentle pressure of the teeth, generally it's more comfortable for him if you cushion your teeth with your lips. Some people suggest the use of a lubricant, but the taste is usually disagreeable; even those flavored massage oils intended for lovers only can make your mouth feel unpleasantly greasy. Your saliva ought to be enough.

Movies like *Deep Throat* have focused a lot of attention on the question of how far inside your mouth your lover's penis can go, and this aspect discourages many women. After one experience that makes them feel like they might gag, they decide they are no good at oral sex and give the whole thing up. In real life, deep-throated heroines who can happily swallow an entire penis

are just as rare as heroes with a nine-inch penis—
and no more necessary to either party's happiness.
If you have a long throat, or a well-controlled
gag reflex, and you find it easy to accept the
entire penis, that's fine. But it's not the goal of
oral sex. Since most of the man's sensations are
concentrated in the head of his penis, it's not all
that important what happens at the base. Take
as much of the penis inside your mouth as feels
comfortable. You can then use your hands on
the remaining part, as well as to continue stimulation of the scrotum and anus.

If you continue to stimulate your lover to the
point of climax, you will be faced with the question of what to do with his ejaculate. For some
reason, this often leads to a real struggle between partners, with the man insisting that it is
a sign of affection to swallow it and the woman
quite unwilling to do any such thing. One therapist has suggested that the act of swallowing a
man's semen is symbolic of accepting his sexual
domination, so perhaps that explains why it can
become such a contest of wills. The wisest course
at action is to do whatever is most pleasurable
for *you*—and to refrain from being drawn into
an argument about it. Treat it as a matter of
personal preference not a political principle.

Anal sex

"Take this job and shove it!"
"You know what you can do with it!"
"Up yours, buddy!"

Since we hear remarks like this coming out of the mouths of men every day, is it any wonder that we have negative associations to anal sex? It is so frequently used as a metaphor for anger, for revenge, for domination, that the act is hard to associate with tenderness, or respect, or love. Therefore women are resistant, or even downright hostile, when men suggest anal sex as part of a lovemaking session.

This attitude is unfortunate, because anal sex has the potential for great stimulation and even greater enjoyment. Women who have tried anal sex often report that they achieve orgasms of great intensity, and some women actually come to prefer it to vaginal sex. As explained in Chapter Seven, there are good physiological reasons for this, since the sensitive skin of the anus and rectum is the same type as that which covers the genitals and is connected to the same nerves. In both men and women, the area is designed to be erotically responsive. What interferes with this response is the fact that many of us are unable to respect this particular part of our own anatomy, and also we fear that it may be painful.

Men tend to be more open-minded on this subject than women, and a surprisingly large number of men would like to make love to their partners anally if they thought their partners would agree. They say they are stimulated by the chance to feel and stroke the buttocks, and they are excited by the tight fit of the anal passage. Although it is certainly rare for a man to want anal sex only, your partner may be very enthusiastic about adding it to your repertoire. Some couples employ it as a provocative preliminary to vaginal intercourse (make sure his penis is washed before he inserts it into your vagina as bacteria from your anus can cause infection); others use it to end a session. Sometimes it is adopted as a solution to a problem: after childbirth, when the vagina may still be a bit sensitive; as a protection against herpes or as a birth-control measure.

If you decide you are willing to try anal sex, here are some things to keep in mind to help make it a pleasurable experience. You might want to choose a "man on top" position—of course, it will be one in which your buttocks are elevated—rather than a "rear entry" position to begin with, since it will allow face-to-face communication and reassure you that you share control of the situation. (Once you are accustomed to anal sex, you may find the rear-entry positions more comfortable.)

Some women fear that anal sex will be a painful experience, but there will be no discomfort as long as their partners exercise a bit of consideration and patience (qualities that are necessary for *any* type of intercourse to feel good). Your partner's insertion should be very slow, giving your rectal muscles time to adjust to the width of the penis. Lubrication is usually needed—and your application of the lubricant to his penis can be an enjoyable part of your preliminary lovemaking. There's no hurry, so take as much time as you need to feel comfortable. Eventually, the ring of muscle tissue will expand to accommodate your partner's penis, and then you will be ready to enjoy the next stage. That consists of the same thrusting motions both of you use in vaginal sex, and it is very likely to end in intense mutual gratification.

It's a good idea for your partner to wash his penis afterward, with warm water and a little soap (or you might enjoy doing it for him). This will prevent any possibility of bacteria invading and infecting his urethra, or yours if you go on to other forms of lovemaking.

You may be surprised by the rewards your willingness to try anal sex can bring. "I agreed only because it was important to Kenny," said Althea. "He had suggested it several times, and finally I felt I had enough trust in him to try. But it turned out that I enjoyed it even more than he did. At the same time he was thrusting, he was able to give me manual stimulation around the clitoris and the vaginal lips, and the feeling was so intense I thought I was going to faint from the pleasure. And of course it was nice to know that Kenny enjoyed it too . . . it was an experience that really brought us closer together."

CHAPTER ELEVEN

Timing

"I thought it was going to be a wonderful evening," said Todd, a computer engineer in Seattle. "We had a leisurely dinner at her place and then lingered over our brandy in front of the fireplace. I was feeling very relaxed and mellow, and the whole night seemed to stretch out in front of us. But when we got to bed, everything changed. She acted like a woman in a big hurry, and she aroused and excited me so quickly that I couldn't control myself. I came just a few minutes after we started making love. The next thing I knew, she had jumped up to take a shower, and suddenly she was out in the kitchen rattling pots and pans as she cleaned up the dirty dishes. The spell was definitely broken. I got dressed and left . . . permanently."

The woman involved in this scenario may still be wondering resentfully why he never called again. What did she do wrong? She was only trying to excite him, to heat him up to fever pitch as quickly as possible and to help him have a fast climax. Isn't that what men really want? Well, maybe that's the way love scenes are written in pornographic books, but in real life, there is an important point about making love that this woman overlooked.

Sexual tension

Human sexual response is based on the accumulation of a specific type of physiological and psychological tension that builds up to be discharged at last in the moment of climax. Therefore, the more tension that accumulates, the greater will be the sense of release.

Imagine that you have a little itch in the middle of your back. Scratch it right away and you can forget all about it. But now suppose that you're sitting in the office of a man who is interviewing you for an important job when the itch strikes. Of course you don't want to make a public spectacle of yourself by twisting your arms around like a contortionist to scratch your back. So you wait, and try to ignore it. The itch simply gets worse and worse, until you become so obsessed by it that you can barely hear what the interviewer is saying to you. And when you finally leave his office and stop in the hallway to scratch that itch at last—ah, what ecstasy!

It is much the same with making love. If you hurry to achieve orgasm (or give your lover one) the minute you feel the least little bit of excitement, it's like scratching a little itch: satisfying but hardly a memorable event in your life. But if you let the tension grow and build . . . it may result in a night both of you remember forever.

Sometimes the circumstances of your relationship provide all the buildup of tension you could ask for. For example, if your lover has been away for several weeks, the time apart from one another contributes to a kind of tension that can make your reunion a very exciting occasion. This same factor can make the early stages of a new relationship the most memorable of its existence, simply because the inevitable uncertainties about whether or when or how you will get together can create similar tensions. A wise woman takes advantage of all these sources of built-in tension—not to be a "tease" who treats her lover unfairly but instead to heighten the pleasant feeling of tension and thereby increase the force of the eventual release. It's good to remember that both psychologically and physiologically, men often thrive on the challenge of an obstacle to be overcome.

But a good long-term relationship usually does not contain these sources of built-in tension; there are no genuine obstacles to quick and easy gratification. When you plan to spend this Wednesday night with Bill, as you do almost every Wednesday, you assume you are going to make love, as you do almost every Wednesday.

It may be nice to look forward to, but it's hardly a source of even the tiniest bit of tension. In such situations, the answer to introducing an element of enhancing tension lies in the *timing* of your lovemaking activity.

No matter how skillfully you have learned to do certain things to one another, if you do them too fast, both you and your partner lose some of the potential pleasure. For most couples, slowing down the process of lovemaking will not only increase the total number of minutes spent in the enjoyment of love, which can't be a bad thing, but also heighten the sensations of love. Enjoy each and every minute, and don't rush like a greedy child to the peak moment of orgasm before you've sampled all the pleasures along the way.

The stop-and-start technique

In Chapter Nine, the stop-and-start technique was introduced as a way you can help your lover maintain ejaculatory control. This technique will also work to help you achieve the goal of increasing sexual tension through timing. Using whatever means you both enjoy, stimulate your lover through a period of rising excitement, until he tells you he is very near his climax (or you discover that fact for yourself).

Then quickly stop all motion entirely until his excitement dies down a bit. These breaks in the action can be a good time to switch from one type of sexual activity to another. For example, you might change positions, or switch from intercourse to oral sex, or let your lover relax blissfully while you give him manual stimulation. Soon he may discover that the new type of stimulation is even more agreeable than the one before, and that may then lead to the need for a new pause.

Some couples like to stretch out the stops even further. They take the time to shower together, or to sip some cold champagne and share a cigarette. You could read your lover a few pages of an erotic book, or give him a relaxing body massage, or listen to some good music. He might enjoy a period of kissing and cuddling, maybe talking—about sex or something else—before resuming sexual activity. Even if you wait so long that he loses part or all of his erection, don't worry; when he hears a new call to action, he will be ready.

Most men agree that three to four of these periods of stop-and-start are optimal, leading eventually to an explosive climax that brings great pleasure. Trying to go on with this pattern for *too* long may make orgasm, when it finally comes, an anticlimax. Don't turn it into a marathon of your lover's endurance!

Is longer always better?

There is only one general rule about sex, and that is, there is no general rule. Each time you make love, you are combining two different individuals who bring to the situation a specific set of physical and emotional responses. So there may be times when you both want your lovemaking to be fast and simple: the proverbial quickie. Still, for most couples most of the time, *slower* is usually better, because it can eventually bring the most intense sensations.

But longer is not necessarily better in and of itself; and some couples' efforts to prolong the time they spend actually having intercourse seem counterproductive. One sex manual advises a man to "think of other things." In India, men who want to be good lovers supposedly train themselves to read books or perform mathematical calculations in their heads while they make love. The value of these practices seems dubious. Although more time may be spent in the act, it is unlikely that more enjoyment comes of it. It's like making love by remote control: his penis is there but the rest of him isn't.

The same holds true for the practice of using numbing ointments or sprays. You can find these in sex shops and even in some well-stocked drugstores. Their active ingredient is a topical anesthetic, like the one in throat sprays that soothe the pain of sore throats or the one the dentist brushes over your gums before he uses a needle to inject novocaine. These ointments simply prevent the man from feeling any sensation in his penis. So the poor dear can thrust away as long as his physical strength permits, without any climax-causing excitement. Or enjoyment. It seems to defeat the whole purpose of the occasion.

Let's do it again

When a man reaches orgasm accompanied by ejaculation, he undergoes immediate physical changes. Respiration, heart beat, and blood pressure all drop, the penis shrinks, and he feels very relaxed, even perhaps sleepy. This phase is called the refractory period, and during this time no amount of sexual stimulation, no matter how expert, can bring another erection and the return of desire. The duration of the refractory period depends on many factors, such as the age, health, and psychological condition of the man, the time elapsed since his last ejaculation, and the general frequency of sexual activity in his life.

But many men—even some of those who fall asleep after they make love—like the idea of an encore before the night (or day) is over. All they need is a little encouragement. One woman passed along her surefire program. "After we make love, I always let him have a little catnap. Then I get up and fix a snack, heating up some wonderful barbecued ribs I bought earlier that day. Sitting at the table stark naked, eating ribs and drinking beer: you have no idea how lascivious that can be! When we finish, we are both so messy we need a bath, so we take turns soaping each other in the nice warm water. By the time we are drying off, he is usually ready to start again."

The time after you make love is when you should use your imagination and indulge your partner (and yourself) in a variety of sensual entertainments: good food or drink, a little massage, relaxing music. After an hour or so, move from the sensual to the more specifically sexual and see how your lover responds. He may be ready to rise to even greater heights, and the intimacy you have enjoyed in the interim will carry over to make your love even more enjoyable.

Coming together

One issue of timing that looms large from some couples is the simultaneous orgasm, with both partners coming at exactly the same moment.

For some reason, this practice was deemed almost a necessity in the sex manuals of the late 1950s and early sixties, and both partners considered themselves failures if they couldn't manage it.

Certainly, there is a strong feeling of shared pleasure in the simultaneous orgasm, and it can be very nice when it happens spontaneously. On the other hand, the effort to make it happen can diminish the pleasure of both partners. The woman may feel under great pressure to match her partner's speed—a pressure that is bound to make her feel less responsive, rather than more. Or the man may feel resentful about the need to hold back when he is really ready to reach orgasm.

Such problems are unnecessary and can easily be solved by abandoning the goal of simultaneous orgasm. "Gary used to insist that we should come at exactly the same moment," says Anita, "but I began to realize it was ruining our relationship. It took such self-control for him to wait for me that he didn't really enjoy making love. So finally I convinced him we should try something different. After a few minutes of making love, he switches to giving me oral sex, until I reach my own climax. We just hold each other close for a while, and then he goes back to making love. We have found that this really works best for us, and it increases the time we spend in lovemaking without requiring inhuman self-discipline from either one of us."

Experiment with your lover to find the ways that work best for the two of you, and don't feel bound by any rules about what should happen when.

CHAPTER TWELVE

When You Run into Problems

When we women imagine a night of love, we always envision the man in question as lusty and eager, begging to be allowed to perform all night. In other words, we are thinking about the *myth* of male sexuality rather than about a specific human being, who might be angry at his boss, or worried about his income taxes, or resentful at being maneuvered into going out to dinner first when he really just wanted to stay home and have a cozy evening for two. So we are surprised (and presumably so is he) when his penis doesn't act like a machine, throbbing away and ready to go to work at a moment's notice. We respond by labeling the situation a "problem," and suddenly the whole room fills up with emotional stress. The entire relationship may be in jeopardy.

What kind of things can go wrong with the male sexual response? First and most drastic is the lack of any noticeable response at all; the man is unable to achieve an erection. Or he may be able to have an erection but loses it before intercourse can begin. Or his erection is only partial, and he never gets hard enough for insertion. This type of problem prevents intercourse from taking place at all (although, of course, there are still some possible avenues of mutual gratification).

A second category of problem is called premature ejaculation. The man achieves a full erection and then becomes so excited so quickly that intercourse is distressingly brief. Some men ejaculate as they are preparing to enter the vagina, others as soon as they enter, others after just a few moments of thrusting. A useful way to think of premature ejaculation is that the man is unable to control his ejaculation as he would like to, thereby diminishing his satisfaction and his partner's pleasure.

A third type of problem is retarded ejaculation, which means that the man is either unable to reach a climax at all, or unable to do so within a reasonable length of time spent in stimulation. Although this problem doesn't, like the others, present a barrier to intercourse, and may enable his partner to achieve a climax, it is nevertheless a difficulty with practical and emotional implications for both parties.

Of course, men are not the only human beings to have something occasionally go wrong with their sexual response. It happens to women too; but for a variety of reasons it creates less of a problem when it does. One obvious reason is that a woman's lack of complete physiological readiness for sex doesn't prevent intercourse. Moreover, she can, if she chooses, disguise the fact, a luxury men don't have. But she may not bother to pretend, because she probably feels much less pressure about the whole situation than he does. It's considered not only acceptable but even normal for women to have unreliable sexual responses; no one expects machinelike regularity from her. To be turned on at one moment and uninterested the next is part of the myth of female sexuality. It is probably no more accurate than the male sexual myths, but at least it provides a lot better shelter in times of trouble.

When you shouldn't try to do it yourself

Since human beings are not machines, even the most virile man may occasionally have some sort of problem when he is making love, and that's the situation this chapter addresses. But if the problem occurs every time he makes love, that's beyond the scope of any book. It's a situation that requires not only the knowledge and skill of a professional, but also the detachment. Sometimes a chronic sexual problem has some physical basis; often it reflects an emotional problem of long standing. For example, psychotherapists suggest that a premature ejaculator may harbor feelings of hostility toward women, seeing them as manipulative and greedy. His lack of ejaculatory control is his passive-aggressive way of paying them back.

If you are involved with a man who has a chronic problem in regard to his sexual response, the best thing you can do is urge him to seek professional help before it damages your relationship beyond repair. In general, sex seems to be an area in which therapy is quite effective, and there are now standard techniques for dealing with premature ejaculation and incomplete or lack of erections. Some therapists prefer to treat the couple as a unit rather than the man alone, and others suggest it as an alternative to the use of sexual surrogates. If you are considering this possibility, it is a good idea to arrange for an appointment of your own with the therapist, so you can find out exactly what will be required of you before you make your final decision. You may find that your participation will bring its own kind of emotional stress to deal with.

Your first reaction

Sooner or later, nearly every woman faces that unpleasant moment when she realizes that her partner is having a problem with his sexual response. The first and most important rule to keep firmly in mind for this moment is *do not take it personally*. Unfortunately, it's all too easy to feel that your partner's lack of response is somehow related to your own lack of appeal. You assume his limp penis is due to that extra piece of cake you ate yesterday, or your failure to get a manicure, or the inadequacy of your deodorant. Ninety-nine percent of the time, there is no validity to these assumptions. So don't blame yourself for the problem. It would happen even if you were one hundred times more attractive, or one hundred times more experienced as a lover. You are not the cause of the problem; it is important to remember that your only concern is not to make it worse by your response.

If you don't take your partner's problem personally, you will also find it easier to follow the second rule of response, which is to avoid getting emotional about the situation yourself. There's already one emotionally distressed person in the room, and things are not going to get better if you make it unanimous. Of course, you may feel disappointed about the way things are going (or not going). And you may be apprehensive about how this is going to affect your relationship. But the best thing you can do at the time is try to appear calm and unemotional. Your goal is to help him solve his problem; once that happens, you will find that yours improves automatically.

A third rule of response is to avoid an inquest

into the problem. It is only natural that men with a problem—and their partners—wonder why it has happened. But trying to dissect the problem on the spot is almost certain to be counterproductive. After all, if the poor man knew the answer to the question, he would no doubt have solved the problem already; it's a problem precisely because there is no clear answer to the question "Why?" Moreover, even if your intentions are purely helpful, asking him to discuss or explain why he has no erection will inevitably sound like an accusation, a subtle form of blame. Don't give in to temptation to analyze the problem.

In fact, a wise and delightful friend, now in her fifties and greatly adored by her boyfriend who is twenty-five years younger, suggests that this is a poor time for much conversation of any sort. "A man with a temporary problem doesn't really want to talk about it at all," she asserts. "No matter how sympathetic you try to be, you are going to wound him by trying to discuss it. You want to tell him about your concern, your understanding, your patience; but at that particular moment they only serve to make him feel worse. He's too embarrassed and upset to be able to deal well with the situation—or you. The best course is to talk as little as possible. Let your actions convey the support and sympathy he doesn't want to hear in words."

Removing the feeling of pressure

The key to solving the problem presented by your partner's temporary lack of response is removing the sense of pressure from the situation. His natural reaction will almost certainly be to try harder and more frantically to get and maintain an erection, but unfortunately, that very desperation will be his own worst enemy. He needs to relax, and so do you. Once that is achieved, he may be able to regain his customary response. And if not, the two of you will still be able to enjoy the time you spend together.

Encourage him to relax by letting him know that you are not concerned over the situation. Remind him that the two of you have plenty of time, and show him that there are lots of ways for a couple to satisfy one another. Don't make a sudden frantic effort to stimulate him yourself, and don't push him to do it to himself. Tell him you'd just like to be close to him for a while, and enjoy the time to cuddle, to stroke him (but don't concentrate on genital areas), and to kiss. Many women complain that they don't get enough of this sort of affectionate contact, so this is a good opportunity to indulge in friendly stroking and fondling. You might also suggest a shower, or a snack, or you might give him a massage; in other words, treat the time like an extended break in a night of successful lovemaking.

Sometimes this relaxation will solve the problem. He will get an erection, and the two of you can go on to the lovemaking session you had originally intended. But sometimes when you resume sexual activity, you find that nothing has changed. In those situations, and also in cases of premature ejaculation where he is unable to achieve a second erection, it is time to suggest (or demonstrate) alternate avenues to sexual satisfaction. It has already been emphasized in this book that a stiff penis is not a prerequisite for happiness—an attitude that will stand you in good stead at this particular moment.

If your partner is unable to achieve an erection, or has already lost it in premature ejaculation, then you can encourage him to satisfy you through oral sex or manual stimulation. Not only does this bring you pleasure, but it is also good for his ego, since it permits him still to view himself as a good partner and a skillful lover. "That was a very special time for us," said Gloria. "At first I thought it was a disaster, when Andrew failed to respond to my caresses. I knew he'd been working hard that month, but I never expected it to affect him like that. Eventually, we both accepted the fact that he wasn't going to get hard, and then he switched his attention to making me happy. Since he wasn't in a hurry, and he was thinking only of my pleasure, he was just wonderful. What he did with his tongue drove me to new heights of feeling! It was easy for him to see what an effect he was having on me, and that made him feel proud. That night brought us a lot closer together, and although the problem has never occurred again, we've incorporated some of what we learned then into our regular approach to making love. Now we take turns concentrating on each other, and we enjoy it even more than before."

Although not every occasion may turn out quite as well as it did for Gloria and Andrew, both of you will benefit from the willingness to use alternate techniques of lovemaking rather than calling it quits just because your partner's penis is not erect. And he may find that the sight of your enjoyment of oral sex or manual stimulation finally brings his own arousal.

What about reciprocating? This is something to check out with your partner. He may find it pleasant to have his penis stroked, licked, and sucked even if he is not erect, as long as he can relax and enjoy it. On the other hand, he may find it irritating, or it may awaken his anxiety about his lack of erection.

Your attitude is the key to success

If you follow these suggestions, you will have avoided turning the situation into a problem with a capital P. Keep your sense of proportion, and you'll see that it is only a temporary obstacle to one specific type of lovemaking. But you can still enjoy each other, and there are plenty of avenues of sexual gratification for you to explore together. And when your partner sees that you are reacting in such a relaxed and matter-of-fact fashion, he will follow suit. And sooner or later, he will find appropriate ways to express his gratitude.

CHAPTER THIRTEEN

Erotic Fun and Games

SET: a bed
ACTORS: one man, one woman
COSTUMES: none
ACTION: straightforward sex

The above is a time-honored scenario for making love, and generations of couples have found it perfectly adequate. But eventually, you may find that it begins to seem just the tiniest little bit boring. That means it's time to inject an element of play and fantasy into your lovemaking.

What do you do with the whipped cream?

"From the things I read, I had the vague idea there were people out there doing bizarre things with ice and bananas, but I never could figure out exactly what it was," laughs Joan. "Once I put a bowl of fruit on the bedside table, but my boyfriend just ate it while we were watching television. What are you supposed to do with that stuff anyway?"

Ice, fruit, whipped cream, and anything else you've heard about are only props you can use to play sexy games. These games don't necessarily drive you to new heights of erotic stimulation, nor do they often make your sexual encounter more intense and passionate. (In fact, in many cases, you may find that what they do is make you giggle helplessly.) But laughter and playfulness make their own contribution to sex, and you may find that sharing some silly experience with whipped cream brings you and your lover much closer together—so later in your lovemaking you really do become much more passionate.

Here are a few ideas for erotic fun and games with easy-to-find props.

1. Try some experiments with crushed ice (not cubes, which are too lumpy). Put a little in your mouth while you are giving your partner oral sex; some men love the titillating alternation of your warm lips and the cold interior of your mouth. It sounds weird, but some men have a similar fondness for the feeling of a little ice inside your vagina. Wrap a small amount of crushed ice in a small handkerchief for insertion, and see how your man responds to this hot-cold combination.

2. To return to the subject of whipped cream . . . It can be applied to any part of either lover's anatomy to encourage friendly licking and sucking: breasts, stomach, buttocks, penis, vaginal lips. The most fun way to put it on is with a spray can (and some men get turned on by the tickle of the foam as it emerges from the can). Gourmets might want to consider other flavorful possibilities: thin chocolate sauce, fruit jam or jelly, maple syrup. . . .

3. Flavored massage oils, which are sold in many stores, can be used as you would any oil for a relaxing body massage. Some couples like to take turns applying it to one another, a sexy little game in itself, and then make love while they're still all slippery. The flavoring—usually strawberry or cinnamon—adds an extra dimension to licking and sucking.

4. Some bright manufacturer has come up with the idea of making edible underwear—really! They're called Candypants, and they are made for both men and women. They come in several sizes and colors, and the men's version even has slightly obscene slogans printed on them. You have to admit there's something amusing about the notion of eating a hole right through your lover's underwear to get to the good parts.

5. Try body paints for some childish

fun that can quickly turn into something more adult. There is a brand made for children to use in the tub that can add some excitement to your shower or bath, as you draw pictures and write messages on each other's bodies. Other brands, more likely to be sold in "adult shops," are flavored so they can be licked off happily (although you will probably still want a shower afterward).

6. Now about that fruit! Yes, Virginia, there are some interesting uses for fruit . . . all it takes is a little imagination. You can substitute beautiful green grapes for the pearls in the age-old entertainment of "pearl diving" in which the man uses his tongue and lips to search the vagina for hidden treasure. Some men also love the thrill of eating a banana this way, searching deeper and deeper for each subsequent bite.

Are there really any "sex aids"?

Every city has its sex shops, and they usually have a section called "Sex aids" or some similar terminology. Don't get your hopes up and expect to find magical devices that will sweep you off to previously unknown heights of sensation. But with a bit of browsing, you and your lover might find something that will add pleasant variety to your lovemaking.

The most frequently purchased device is probably the vibrator. Of course, some women buy them to use when they are alone, but they can play a part in couple sex as well. Your lover can use a vibrator to stimulate you as a preliminary to intercourse, or he can use it as additional stimulation while he is giving you oral sex. Some men like to use it around the clitoral area during anal sex, and others use it on the buttocks and anus during vaginal sex. Remember that turnabout is fair play; your partner might enjoy being on the receiving end of all this stimulation. You can use it on his buttocks and anus and (with a light touch) on the scrotum as well. And experiment to see whether he likes it on the penis . . . and if so, where.

Vibrators come in a variety of shapes and sizes. Most familiar is probably the penile shape, but it might be tactful to avoid this one when you are selecting a vibrator to use with a partner. You don't want to imply that the vibrator is a rival—bigger and harder and battery-equipped— to his penis. The spoon shape or disk shape would be a better choice, because it will be easier for your lover to regard it as an adjunct to his own powers, rather than a substitute for them.

Another frequently used sex aid is a device that slips over the erect penis. One such gadget is the cock ring, a hard rubber ring (rather like the ones babies are given to teethe on) that slides down to the base of the penis after erection. It is popularly thought to be a help in maintaining an erection, but it is more accurate to say that it merely slows down the process of deflation, by slightly constricting the veins through which the blood flows back into the body. Its other function is to stimulate the clitoral area with each thrust of the penis (usually this is done by the softer flesh-covered pubic bone). It's doubtful whether a cock ring really does much for either one of you physiologically, but it certainly might provide psychological stimulation, which is just as important. Some men view such devices as a kind of armor that makes the penis downright invincible—and that's certainly a good attitude to bring to lovemaking!

There are also various rubber sheaths meant to cover the shaft of the penis; they usually look something like fancy condoms that have the end cut off. Some are covered by patterns of ridges of thicker rubber, others with tiny little rubberized spikes. These (often called French ticklers) are intended to increase the sensation the woman feels during thrusting, and they probably work best when they are in contact with the sensitive skin around the vaginal lips rather than inside the vagina itself, where there are relatively few nerve endings to pick up such sensations.

Some sex shops put out catalogs, illustrating and describing these and other sex aids. The truth of the matter is that you and your lover may well get more enjoyment out of looking at the catalog together and imagining how you *might* use such things than you would out of actually employing them. Physiologically, the parts nature designed for lovemaking are completely functional without any additional assistance. But psychologically, the idea—or the sex aid—may provide a bit of stimulation you will both enjoy.

Make it a costume affair

There's certainly nothing wrong with nudity, but sometimes clothes—or costumes—can be every bit as exciting. An earlier chapter mentioned the effect lingerie can have on the male imagination, for example. Try wearing a sexy nightgown or a lacy camisole to bed; or a garter belt with black stockings, and nothing else. You might also consider the lingerie manufacturers' version of a fig leaf, the G-string. One of my friends bought several pairs of crotchless panties at a shop that seemed to cater mainly to strippers: one pair is black with red lace trim around the crotchless "target" and she says these never fail to delight her lover. Her latest discovery is the effect of wearing them with a pair of old-fashioned black stockings that reach just to midthigh and are held up by a pair of bright red garters.

But don't stop with lingerie, and don't concentrate only on yourself. Black leather, for instance . . . you might wear a leather jacket, with nothing on underneath, or you might give him a pair of black leather underpants (they make them with a strategically placed hole for his penis!). Or try his-and-hers silk kimonos; a demure little-girl's pinafore; a feather boa; a hip-length fuzzy sweater; an elegant caftan for him. All it takes is letting your imagination run wild as you look at the clothes in your closet or the lingerie department of a store.

The use of fantasy

Dressing up in costumes may be part of a larger drama, as you and your lover act out a favorite fantasy. For example, he may want you to buy a white nurse's uniform, to be used in his fantasy of being a patient who is seduced by a nurse as he lies helpless in bed. Or he may like to see you dressed as a teenage schoolgirl while he plays the part of the principal. Or perhaps he wants you to don a big wig and remove your clothes like a stripper.

Acting out a fantasy can be an overwhelmingly erotic sensation; but it can also be annoying or repulsive to a partner who doesn't share it. It's a good idea to talk it over first, to make sure you understand just what he has in mind when he says he wants to play doctor. Ask him to describe a favorite fantasy (he might be more comfortable calling it a dream, or a story he read or heard from someone else). If the general idea seems agreeable to you, you can then surprise him next time with the props and a scenario for acting it out. But don't undertake it if the notion strikes you as threatening, embarrassing, or "kinky"; fantasies only work when they are mutually agreeable.

One type of fantasy that has a surprisingly widespread appeal involves "bondage and discipline," in which one partner pretends to force the other into sexual submission. The operative word here is "pretend" since this should *never* be a genuine coercion. But if you both find the idea provocative, you might try it. A common practice is to tie either the arms or legs, or sometimes both, to the bedpost (for psychological security, use thin cord and simple knots, so the bound partner knows it will be easy to escape). Then you virtually assault the temporarily helpless person with love. The "discipline" part is another form of pretended coercion, that includes gentle spankings with the hand, a hairbrush, or a towel—just enough to cause a slight sting.

You and your partner may enjoy dreaming up your own fantasies as a way of adding a happy sense of play to your lovemaking. Some couples like to pretend they just met; others imagine themselves in exotic settings or unusual circumstances. As long as you both enjoy it . . . well, why not?

CHAPTER FOURTEEN

Some Special Secrets

In the course of the interviews for this book, both men and women confided some of their own special secrets of successful lovemaking. These ideas won't work for everybody, but you might find something here that will spark your imagination!

1. It is said that when Napoleon knew he would be able to get a few nights off from the war, he sent a special courier to Josephine to tell her he was coming—and to warn her not to take a bath. Some men are strongly turned on by a woman's natural body odor, and greatly prefer it to the scent of soap and deodorant and perfume. Research indicates that humans, like many other animals, do in fact secrete chemicals called pheromones that are designed to be sexually attractive to the opposite sex—so you might consider giving yours a chance!

2. According to the ancient Chinese charts used by acupuncturists, the area of the body

linked to sexual response is the very top of the heel, just below the Achilles tendon. So you might incorporate into your preliminary stroking some concentrated massage of the feet and ankles, with a special focus on this sensitive area. Your lover will certainly benefit from the relaxation, and he may respond healthily to the stimulation.

3. Practice this "sexercise," called the Kegel, after the gynecologist who developed it for his patients, for ten to fifteen minutes every day. Imagine that your lover's penis is inside you and try to embrace it with a big squeeze, as if you're trying to stop from urinating. This contracts a ring of muscle just inside the vagina. Hold the squeeze to the count of ten, then relax to the count of five. With repeated practice, the muscle will eventually become strong enough for you to be able to create some interesting new sensations for your lover when he is really inside you.

4. Many men find it very erotic to watch—and occasionally participate in—a woman's private rituals to prepare for going to bed. Give him the pleasure of watching you undress while he sips his brandy in a comfortable chair, and don't forget to ask for his help with the buttons at the back of your dress, or the fastener of your necklace. But don't stop with taking off

your clothes. Sit at your dressing table and re-move your earrings. Brush your hair slowly and carefully . . . and give him a chance to participate. Smooth lotion over your shoulders, arms, legs. Spray yourself with perfume. Dust yourself with powder from a fluffy puff. As he plays the role of secret observer of these time-honored femi-nine rituals, he will feel more and more mascu-line . . . and in this situation, that's a definite advantage.

5. Whip your lover with feathers. Sally has an arrangement of feathers in a vase on her bed-side table; it's a nice decorative note but it's also functional. She selects a feather and goes to work on her lover: stroking him all over, tick-ling and teasing. It's very effective on the buttocks, scrotum, and even the penis itself.

6. Before you begin to make love, agree on the rules of a game to play with your lover: the first one to reach a climax *loses*. (Make the prize for the winner something interesting.) Each person's efforts to avoid the inevitable cause the tension to build and build, and the final plea-sure becomes that much more attractive and enjoyable.

7. Choose a position for lovemaking that al-lows you to reach your lover's feet. (A sitting "rear entry" position is a good choice, or you

can try "woman on top" with your head facing toward his feet. Or you can use this suggestion during oral sex rather than genital intercourse, since that makes it relatively easy to find a convenient position.) When you can feel that your lover is starting to ejaculate, reach out and gently pull his toes, especially the big toe. This extension of the foot and leg muscles heightens the sensation of release.

8. Men love to see the transformation of a woman from prim to passionate (and perhaps to believe they are the cause of it all!). Blow his mind by dressing very formally, in an outfit that conceals every inch of your skin—and then let him discover that you are wearing Frederick's of Hollywood underwear underneath. The contrast makes you seem especially sexy.

9. Surprise your lover by making a reservation for the two of you to spend an hour in a hot tub at a local spa, health club, or sauna. You'll get a private room with a big tub and lots of hot water ... and the time to do whatever comes into your mind. Begin with a slow massage to work out all the muscle stress and strain, and then move on to something sexier. The combination of the water and the heat can be very erotic.

10. Some men become very aroused by overtones of almost combative aggressiveness. They

love a wrestling match, for example, that starts out as straightforward competition and eventually turns into lovemaking. Another possibility is a pillow fight; if you can arrange outdoor privacy, you might battle each other with spray from the hose (indoors, you can substitute the fizz from a soft-drink bottle, or champagne showers if you can afford it). As he unleashes a bit of his aggression, he may become very turned on.

11. Here's an idea that Carole Lombard reportedly used to arouse her husband, Clark Gable. Before you begin to make love, use a strong mint-flavored mouthwash. When the sensitive skin on the head of the penis comes in contact with your minty mouth, it will cause an exciting tingle that is very stimulating.

12. Give your man a chance to *look* as well as touch. Either because they are shy, or they are self-conscious about their bodies, many women never really allow their partners to look as much as they'd like to. Several men commented in interviews about what a turn-on it was for them when a woman gave them enough time—and enough light—to see and appreciate her body, and especially the genital area. Don't pass up this chance to create pleasure for both of you just because you are worried that your body isn't perfect.

*   *   *

13. Whip out your Polaroid camera and ask your lover to pose nude for you. He may be shy at first, but your appreciative attitude will soon get him into the spirit of the occasion, as you pretend to be snapping a centerfold for *Playgirl*. Don't be afraid to suggest very sexy . . . even kinky . . . poses once he begins to feel relaxed; it's a good way to introduce fantasies that the two of you can proceed to act out!

CHAPTER FIFTEEN

Putting It All Together

Perhaps you've been wondering as you've read chapter after chapter of suggestions about how to please a man, "But what's in it for me? Am I supposed to be a doormat, existing only to please some man? What about my own pleasure?"

This book deals with the subject of *giving*. Obviously, any relationship in which one person is doing all the giving and one all the taking is not likely to last very long; the urge to give will eventually dry up if it is not encouraged by some signs of reciprocity. With any luck, the man you have chosen as your partner, the man on the receiving end of your own creativity and consideration and willingness to give, is capable of similar generosity of spirit. That means your willingness to please him will be matched by a similar willingness on his part.

But no matter how the man in your scenario responds, it is still true that giving can be its own reward. Many women worry about being "used" by men, but a woman who gives of herself generously and freely, because she wants to confer pleasure on her partner, can never be used, because she is not expecting anything in return but her own pleasure in giving. If you make love to a man because you secretly hope he will marry you, or anyway fall in love with you—or at the very least, call you again next week—then you leave yourself open to being used by men who will seem to make those promises and then fail to carry them out. But if you make love to him because you want to offer him the gift of several hours (or days!) of shared pleasure, then his willingness to accept your gift can't possibly be a form of exploitation.

Selfishness in love, as in many other aspects of life, brings its own downfall. Try to imagine what it would be like to make love to a man when all you are thinking about is what he is going to do for you; surely the very selfishness of your concern would defeat any possibility of pleasure. The same is true if you are trying suspiciously to measure the exact amount of pleasure each of you has given and received, to make sure the accounts balance perfectly.

No, the truth of the matter is that you get the most pleasure yourself when you are in a giving frame of mind. The nice thing about mutuality in lovemaking is that you really do double your pleasure, since you get to enjoy all of your own sensations and also all of his. But that only happens when you give willingly and freely, with no secret strings attached.

Concentrate on the moment

Perhaps the best single piece of advice on the subject of lovemaking is to *concentrate*. Concentrate on the feedback of your own senses: notice how things feel, taste, smell. Concentrate on the moment you are together; don't let yourself be distracted by thoughts of the business meeting you had earlier in the day, or the conversation you want to have with your lover later about that vacation in Bermuda. Most of all, concentrate on the man you are with. Notice how *he* feels and responds. Listen to his breathing. Hear his heart beating. Watch his eyes; feel his skin; *share* his feelings.

Concentrating on the moment will allow you to enjoy a myriad of subtle feelings, and it will prevent you from making the mistake of turning your lovemaking into a race to the finish. There is an unfortunately widespread assumption that sex is nothing more than the search for as many orgasms as quickly as possible through the "magic" of intercourse. That's *one* type of sexual experience, but it's not the only one. There are pleasantly diffuse feelings of low-level sexual arousal that can also be enjoyable; and both men and women may sometimes find that they prefer not to reach orgasm, or at least not as the only reason to make love.

"Ron and I used to think that whenever we

touched each other, we had to take it all the way to making love and having an orgasm, but lately, we've tried to stop being so goal-oriented," says Lisa. "Now sometimes we cuddle and stroke each other without going any farther, and Ron has admitted to himself that he isn't a machine that is always eager to pump away in mindless intercourse. One night last week, after he'd had a long hard day at the office, we went to bed and just held each other until we began to relax. Eventually, I started to stroke his penis gently, and he had an erection, but I just continued the gentle strokes and soon he fell fast asleep. He woke up the next morning in a wonderful mood, happy and rested, and our lovemaking that night was very passionate—but later we agreed that *both* nights had been good ones, each in a different way." If you learn to concentrate on the moment, as Ron and Lisa are doing, you will multiply the number of ways you can enjoy one another, instead of limiting yourself to just one pattern of making love.

Enjoy the whole experience

In a best-selling novel, when the heroine finally gets together with the man of her dreams, the occasion is characterized by some passionate dialogue, followed by even more passionate lovemaking, and then a fade-out. In real life, things rarely work out this way. Over dinner, he spills sauce on his tie and you make enough noise eating your lettuce to wake everyone on the block. You don't know whether to take your clothes off when you go into the bedroom or leave them on and let him worry about it. He gets a cramp in his leg and has to hop around the room until he works it out; you are worried that your period might be starting. When you try a new position, you can't seem to get the required parts together; just as he is thrusting away vigorously, he misses the target altogether.

It may seem to you that these awkward realities spoil the romantic occasion; but the truth of the matter is that reality can be much more interesting, much more exciting, and much more rewarding than fantasy or fiction. One reason is that it puts you in contact with the whole person who is your partner, instead of allowing him to remain a depersonalized phallic symbol. You laugh together, work out solutions to the problems together, and learn something about one another's personalities. This doesn't necessarily mean that you have to fall madly in love with one another, but it does mean that you will be aware of sharing your time and feelings with another human being—and that will make it a richer experience. Making love is first and foremost a form of communication, and the communication should encompass the entire experience the two of you are sharing. It is its very reality that makes it so moving and memorable.

About the Author

Judith Davis is a professional writer living and working in New York. She is the author of *Shape Up for Sex* (Avon, 1979), a book of exercises; and *Queen* (Proteus, 1981) a biography of the rock group.

ASK THE EXPERTS

☐ **WHAT MEN REALLY WANT by Herb Goldberg, Ph.D.** What do men want in a relationship? Why is he afraid to commit? A fresh new approach to communication and understanding between the sexes, this is the definitive guide to love and intimacy in the 1990's.   (169727—$4.99)

☐ **COLD FEET: WHY MEN WON'T COMMIT by Sonya Rhodes and Dr. Marlin S. Potash.** This groundbreaking book offers fascinating insight into the dynamics behind men who both crave and fear intimacy—and tells you what you can do about it!
(159101—$4.99)

☐ **LOVELIVES:** *How We Make Love* **by Samuel Dunkell, M.D.** After you read this revealing book, you can be sure you'll know everything about intimacy, spontenaity, physicality, commitment, and pleasure in your love relationship. (127161—$3.95)

☐ **MAKING LOVE: A WOMAN'S GUIDE by Judith Davis.** What does a man *really* want, anyway? You'll find all the answers in this one book that tells you how to turn your man on, including 20 sure-fire turn-ons to seduce him so he stays seduced; scores of gloriously imaginative ideas in the art of making love memorable; the well-known secret that kindles the steamiest sensual thrills; plus much, much more.
(168224—$4.99)

☐ **WOMEN MEN LOVE/WOMEN MEN LEAVE: WHAT MAKES MEN WANT TO COMMIT by Dr. Connell Cowan and Dr. Melvyn Kinder.** From the bestselling authors of *Smart Women, Foolish Choices* comes this indispensible guide to the puzzling patterns of a man's needs, fears, expectations and—yes!—commitment.   (166418—$5.99)

Prices slightly higher in Canada

Buy them at your local bookstore or use this convenient coupon for ordering.

NEW AMERICAN LIBRARY
P.O. Box 999, Bergenfield, New Jersey 07621

Please send me the books I have checked above.
I am enclosing $_____ (please add $2.00 to cover postage and handling).
Send check or money order (no cash or C.O.D.'s) or charge by Mastercard or
VISA (with a $15.00 minimum). Prices and numbers are subject to change without
notice.

Card #_____ Exp. Date _____
Signature_____
Name_____
Address_____
City _____ State _____ Zip Code _____
For faster service when ordering by credit card call **1-800-253-6476**
Allow a minimum of 4-6 weeks for delivery. This offer is subject to change without notice.

Ⓞ **SIGNET** ⓜ **MENTOR**

HELPFUL GUIDES
(0451)

☐ **HUSBANDS AND WIVES:** *Exploding Marital Myths/Deepening Love and Desire* **by Dr. Cornell Dowan and Dr. Melvyn Kinder.** The best-selling authors of *Smart Women/Foolish Choices* examine marital disenchantment and offer real hope and workable solutions for enriching and enlivening relationships. "Straightforward and sympathetic."—*Publishers Weekly* (162994—$4.99)

☐ **FEELING GOOD: The New Mood Therapy by David Burns, M.D.** This one-of-a-kind integrated approach to depression introduces the principles of Cognitive Therapy, which illustrate that by changing the way we think we can alter our moods and get rid of depression. (167767—$5.99)

☐ **INTIMATE CONNECTIONS by David D. Burns, M.D.** In this breakthrough book, Dr. David Burns, author of the bestselling *Feeling Good*, applies the proven principles of Cognitive Therapy to eliminating the negative thinking and low self-esteem that cause loneliness and shyness, and shows you how to make close friends and find a loving partner. (148452—$5.99)

☐ **BORN TO WIN: Transactional Analysis with Gestalt Experiments by Muriel James and Dorothy Jongeward.** This landmark bestseller has convinced millions of readers that they were **Born to Win!** "Enriching, stimulating, rewarding . . . for anyone interested in understanding himself, his relationships with others and his goals."—*Kansas City Times* (165217—$5.99)

☐ **OVERCOMING PROCRASTINATION by Albert Ellis, Ph.D. and William J. Knaus, Ed.D.** The scientifically proven techniques of Rational-Motive Therapy are applied to procrastination (delaying tactics, frustration, and self-disgust). Examines the causes of procrastination, and the links between procrastination and obesity, drugs, depression, and sexual dysfunction, and other personality and health problems. (159314—$4.50)

Prices slightly higher in Canada

Buy them at your local bookstore or use this convenient coupon for ordering.

NEW AMERICAN LIBRARY
P.O. Box 999, Bergenfield, New Jersey 07621

Please send me the books I have checked above.
I am enclosing $_____ (please add $2.00 to cover postage and handling).
Send check or money order (no cash or C.O.D.'s) or charge by Mastercard or VISA (with a $15.00 minimum). Prices and numbers are subject to change without notice.

Card #_____ Exp. Date _____
Signature_____
Name_____
Address_____
City _____ State _____ Zip Code _____

For faster service when ordering by credit card call **1-800-253-6476**

Allow a minimum of 4-6 weeks for delivery. This offer is subject to change without notice.

EXPERT ADVICE

☐ **CREATIVE DIVORCE by Mel Krantzler.** This nationally acclaimed bestseller has helped thousands of men and women to build new lives in the wake of loneliness, guilt, anger, rejection, and a sense of failure. It offers a positive program for accepting your divorce as a solution, not a punishment, and for reaching out toward new, healthier relationships. "Excellent!" —*Publishers Weekly* (154444—$5.99)

☐ **CREATIVE AGGRESSION by Dr. George R. Bach and Dr. Herb Goldberg.** Suppressing healthy aggression can create frustration, anger, and conflict. This groundbreaking book teaches you how to use aggression for the kind of honest communication that makes personal relationships more intimate and fulfilling. "Engrossing."—*Kirkus Reviews* (161475—$4.95)

☐ **HUMAN BE-ING: How to Have a Creative Relationship Instead of a Power Struggle by William V. Pietsch.** "Here at last is a guide that lets you almost instantly identify your problems and see how to solve them. Here is a work of insight and understanding that will begin to help you from its opening pages to its final chapter."—George O'Neill, co-author of **Open Marriage** (167686—$5.95)

☐ **LOVE AND ADDICTION by Stanton Peale with Archie Brodsky.** This provocative book focuses on interpersonal relationships to explore what addiction really is—psychologically, socially, and culturally. "A rare book, like **Future Shock** and **The Pursuit of Loneliness**, that is destined to become a classic!"—*Psychology Today* (155386—$4.99)

☐ **LIVING AND LOVING AFTER DIVORCE by Catherine Napolitane with Victoria Pellegrino.** Yes, there *is* life after divorce, and this book offers lots of practical advice on how to enjoy it. Includes helpful tips on lawyers and alimony, overcoming loneliness, meeting new people, and much, much more. (149882—$4.95)

Prices slightly higher in Canada

Buy them at your local bookstore or use this convenient coupon for ordering.

NEW AMERICAN LIBRARY
P.O. Box 999, Bergenfield, New Jersey 07621

Please send me the books I have checked above.
I am enclosing $_____ (please add $2.00 to cover postage and handling). Send check or money order (no cash or C.O.D.'s) or charge by Mastercard or VISA (with a $15.00 minimum). Prices and numbers are subject to change without notice.

Card #_____ Exp. Date _____
Signature_____
Name_____
Address_____
City _____ State _____ Zip Code _____

For faster service when ordering by credit card call **1-800-253-6476**

Allow a minimum of 4-6 weeks for delivery. This offer is subject to change without notice.